ICETE Series

Integration

There are few more challenging issues in training people for Christian ministry than the transformative integration of head, heart, and hand. We can know good things, feel good things, and do good things: but they need to be integrated in our lives and ministries, not disintegrated! David Wright's book helpfully names the problem, points to the Bible to find the way forward, and gives practical advice on how to achieve it. May many follow where David has led the way.

Peter Adam, PhD
Former Principal,
Ridley College, Melbourne, Australia

The early claim in this very interesting work – that despite a sustained interest in the integration of objectives in theological education for some time, there is a lack of biblical reflection on the issue – is surely true. This book, developed from a PhD thesis re-written with the intent to inform the training of men and women to love and serve God, goes a long way towards redressing that lack. Wright usefully surveys the work done in the area of integration so far and demonstrates the valuable contribution to the debate of the letters to Timothy and Titus as to both content and process. The book ends with eight excellent principles to promote and guide integration in theological education and then some practical ways ahead, not least that faculty should pursue and display integration in their own lives and teaching ministry. This is the richest study of the subject I have read. Theological education would be greatly blessed if it were read by teachers and discussed by faculties, across the world.

Graham Cheesman, PhD
Honourary Lecturer,
Queens University, Belfast, Northern Ireland

One is led to ask "why hasn't someone looked at the link between the letters to Timothy and Titus and theological education theory and practice in this sort of detail before?" But they haven't, and I commend David for doing so. He has approached his research with academic rigour, strong biblical connection, and an earthed pastoral formation focus. *Integration* is well-positioned to be a readable, appreciated discussion partner for those navigating the challenging but fulfilling task of equipping Christian leaders in ways which demonstrate coherence between theological values, character formation, and ministerial skills development.

Allan Harkness, PhD
Founding Dean,
Asia Graduate School of Theology Alliance, Malaysia

A timely, seminal contribution! Wright is issuing a clarion call for the integration of the theological education endeavour that continues to wrestle with multiple forms of divides and, even more so in the escalating crises due to the Covid-19 pandemic. No doubt, this book will be savoured by theological educators and ministry trainers who genuinely seek the formation of the whole people of God. This book is pivotal in making significant biblical reflections on 1 and 2 Timothy and Titus, thought-provoking in engaging with the global scholarship, and renewing in its analyses of the processes and principles of integration. A vital resource, which will surely inspire kingdom-concerned educators to realize ways in which the current practitioners of theological education should embrace change with authentic biblical understanding!

Jessy Jaison, PhD
Director of Research and Advancement
New India Bible Seminary, Kerala, India

The task of providing appropriate ways of developing "faithful people" for Christian service or scholarship has been daunting for theologians and educators. Wright has produced a book that has added a critical yet biblically and theologically sound voice to the task of integration. In his work he presents a framework to many of us who are in such a situation. Reading this book presents hope and a path towards becoming the teachers Christ wants us to be.

John Jusu, PhD
Lecturer,
Africa International University, Nairobi, Kenya

Implementing integration is challenging because of the lack of definitions about what is meant by integration, what is being integrated, describing the nature of learning, and the lack of measures for such learning. Given this ambiguity, this is a timely book for evangelicals since it provides a biblical basis for holistic development, in a time when there is an explosion of knowledge, and some pedagogical intervention is needed. This book provides helpful ways to think about integration using biblical insights from Paul's letters to Timothy and Titus, insights that should be deepened and embedded in practice. More books of this kind are needed, to make a commitment to support student learning for meaningful theological education.

Marilyn Naidoo, PhD
Professor in Practical Theology,
University of South Africa, Pretoria, South Africa
Editor of *Making Connections: Integrative Theological Education in Africa*

This is a remarkable book. It addresses the issue of integration, one of the key challenges in theological education, and it makes a contribution beyond what has been said so far. The argument is based on solid exegetical work. This biblical foundation is the core contribution of the book. It is undoubtedly highly relevant for the development of theological education.

Bernhard Ott, PhD
Chairman, European Council for Theological Education
Faculty, European School of Culture and Theology, Korntal, Germany

Integration and theological education are complex topics, and Wright navigates well through the growing body of literature, creating helpful summaries, critiques, and taxonomies for analysis as well as identifying gaps and making some original proposals. Especially refreshing is his work in the epistles of Timothy and Titus, as he successfully identifies principles and practices that inject new elements into the "growing pains" of the developing discourse around global theological education.

Marvin Oxenham, PhD
Programme Leader Theological Education,
London School of Theology, UK

David Wright has done the global church a great service by providing such a clear, compelling, and – above all – *biblically informed* vision of theological education as part of God's purposes for his church. In this very readable work Dr. Wright brings the careful exegesis of Paul's letters to Timothy and Titus into dialogue the full range of theories concerning theological education today. The result is not only enlightening and challenging, but also *genuinely refreshing to the soul*. This book is a must-read for anyone involved in training others for Christian ministry – or indeed, for anyone who simply believes that the bible should not only be normative for the *content* of our ministry formation, but also normative for the *shape* of that formation. I was privileged to have Dr. Wright as my ministry supervisor many years ago in Australia, and I am delighted to still be learning from him as I train and mentor others for ministry in Southern Africa.

Mike Roe, PhD
Lecturer,
George Whitefield College, Cape Town, South Africa

Helping students to integrate what they learn into their lives continues to be a real challenge for theological education today. How are academic studies and practical learning to be integrated? In this engaging book, David Wright draws on the letters to Timothy and Titus to help us to think more deeply about this question of the integration of theology, skills, and character in theological education. Since these three Pauline Letters say so much about godly character, leadership, training, personal example, ethics, and mission, Wright's work leads to much wisdom and insight about ways to enhance integration in theological education. He also gives an excellent discussion and critique of current thinking about overcoming the perceived fragmentation of theory and practice in theological education, and concludes with eight principles that inform the content and practice of integration, as well as a practical proposal for a way ahead. This invaluable book is a must-read for anyone interested in theological education today!

Paul Trebilco, PhD
Professor of New Testament Studies,
University of Otago, Dunedin, New Zealand

ICETE Series

Integration

A Conversation between Theological Education and the Letters to Timothy & Titus

David C. Wright

© 2022 David C. Wright

Published 2022 by Langham Global Library
An imprint of Langham Publishing
www.langhampublishing.org

Langham Publishing and its imprints are a ministry of Langham Partnership

Langham Partnership
PO Box 296, Carlisle, Cumbria, CA3 9WZ, UK
www.langham.org

ISBNs:
978-1-83973-589-9 Print
978-1-83973-631-5 ePub
978-1-83973-633-9 PDF

David C. Wright has asserted his right under the Copyright, Designs and Patents Act, 1988 to be identified as the Author of this work.

All rights reserved. No part of this publication may be reproduced, stored in a retrieval system or transmitted, in any form or by any means, electronic, mechanical, photocopying, recording or otherwise, without the prior written permission of the publisher or the Copyright Licensing Agency.

Requests to reuse content from Langham Publishing are processed through PLSclear. Please visit www.plsclear.com to complete your request.

Unless otherwise stated, Scripture quotations are from the New Revised Standard Version Bible, copyright © 1989 National Council of the Churches of Christ in the United States of America. Used by permission. All rights reserved.

Scripture quotations marked ESV are from The Holy Bible, English Standard Version® (ESV®), copyright © 2001 by Crossway, a publishing ministry of Good News Publishers. Used by permission. All rights reserved.

Scripture quotations marked HCSB are taken from the Holman Christian Standard Bible®, Copyright © 1999, 2000, 2002, 2003, 2009 by Holman Bible Publishers. Used by permission. Holman Christian Standard Bible®, Holman CSB®, and HCSB® are federally registered trademarks of Holman Bible Publishers.

Scripture quotations marked NASB are taken from the New American Standard Bible®, Copyright © 1960, 1962, 1963, 1968, 1971, 1972, 1973, 1975, 1977, 1995 by The Lockman Foundation. Used by permission.

Scripture quotations marked NIV are taken from the Holy Bible, New International Version®, NIV®. Copyright © 1973, 1978, 1984, 2011 by Biblica, Inc.™ Used by permission of Zondervan.

Scripture quotations marked NKJV are taken from the New King James Version (NKJV). Copyright © 1982 by Thomas Nelson, Inc. Used by permission. All rights reserved.

British Library Cataloguing-in-Publication Data
A catalogue record for this book is available from the British Library

ISBN: 978-1-83973-589-9

Cover & Book Design: ProjectLuz.com

Langham Partnership actively supports theological dialogue and an author's right to publish but does not necessarily endorse the views and opinions set forth here or in works referenced within this publication, nor can we guarantee technical and grammatical correctness. Langham Partnership does not accept any responsibility or liability to persons or property as a consequence of the reading, use or interpretation of its published content.

Contents

Acknowledgements xi

Part A: The Current Scene

1 Grappling with Integration 3

2 Current Voices on Integration 11

Part B: Integration in the Letters to Timothy & Titus

3 What Is Integrated in 1 Timothy? 35

4 What Is Integrated in 2 Timothy and Titus? 53

5 The Process of Integration in the Letters to Timothy and Titus 77

Part C: Looking Forward

6 Integration in the Light of the Letters to Timothy and Titus 101

7 Eight Principles for Integration in Theological Education 119

8 A Possible Way Ahead 135

Bibliography 155

Acknowledgements

First things first: coming from a confessional perspective, I find it only right and proper to thank the God and Father of our Lord Jesus Christ for his grace and mercy in adopting me into his family. Throughout the process of study and writing, he has answered my prayers in many ways. All thanks and praise to him. I would also like to thank my wife, Jacqui, and our children, Andrew, Hannah, and Ben, for their love and support. It is a great blessing to share life with you.

This book flows out of my doctoral studies which began under the supervision of Dr. Andrew Reid with assistance from Dr. Katy Davis. When Andrew was unable to continue because of his ministry commitments, Dr. Peter Adam kindly stepped into the role of supervisor. I am so thankful to God for his provision of Peter, who is humble and gracious with the right blend of encouragement and academic rigour. He and Dr. Brian Rosner, my co-supervisor, made a wonderfully complementary team and I benefited enormously from their input. Thank you, Peter and Brian. I also thank my examiners, Allan Harkness, Paul Trebilco, and Adam White, for their insightful and astute feedback. Their comments undoubtedly sharpened my work and I have incorporated many of their suggestions.

This book would not have been possible without the help of librarians. Barbara Cooper at Bible College SA has been generous in her efforts to track down books and chapters for me, and Rod Benson and the team at Moore College were supportive in a similar way. And the library team at the Australian Lutheran College (Sara Altmann, Lavinia Gent, Shaun Lancaster, Trevor Schaefer) provided a great environment for research and writing.

I am very thankful for the support of my friends and colleagues at Bible College SA, especially Tim Patrick, Mark Kulikovsky, Chris Fresch, Luke Wisley, and Suzie Smith. Thank you to Brinda Ghose for turning my diagrams into something presentable; to Kim Folland, Kathy Fopp, and Rebecca Vincent for their administrative work; and to Mandy Kreuger for her enthusiastic promotional work.

And a huge thank you to the team at Langham! Mark Arnold seamlessly picked up the reins from Vivian Doub's initial work, and I am very grateful for their management of the project. It is a pleasure to work with you. Thank you to those who provided feedback, and to the proofreaders, copy-editors, typesetters, designers, and marketers – it takes a team! Thank you also to Riad Kassis and Michael Ortiz for your willingness to support this work.

I never expected to end up serving in theological education, so it prompted me to seriously examine the training I had received and what we are currently doing. I count it an enormous privilege to help prepare people for ministry in the service of the Lord Jesus, and a joy to do it with the student body of Bible College SA.

Finally, thanks to Gibbo for pushing me through first-year Greek. Who would have thought . . . !

Part A

The Current Scene

1

Grappling with Integration

Most people in vocational ministry reach a crisis point. Perhaps it is a personal tragedy, or a lack of spiritual and numerical growth in the congregation, or conflict in the church that saps all emotional strength; doubts, depression, and despair come the way of most servants of the gospel at one time or another. For me, that crisis point seemed like a crisis season that ran for a number of years.

But as the saying goes, do not waste a crisis! I never expected to be serving the Lord in theological education. My natural inclination had always been towards local-church ministry, and I was hardly a first-class honours student. When I found myself with the responsibility and privilege of training others for ministry, I was forced to do some soul-searching. What gaps had the crisis exposed in me and the formation I had received? Even though I had sat under excellent professors and worked with godly and gifted pastors, why did I feel so ill-equipped for ministry? Why had I failed? And how do we equip the upcoming generation of gospel workers for ministry in such a rapidly changing world? Training students, combined with further study, has provided me with the opportunity to explore, experiment, and think about the issue of integration.

What is integration? There is broad agreement across theological education that the content or inputs of integration are theology, practical skills, and godly character. The International Council for Evangelical Theological Education (ICETE) states in its Manifesto that theological education "must combine spiritual and practical with academic objectives in one holistic integrated educational approach."[1] This international perspective on integration is endorsed by authors writing in a variety of cultural contexts: Graham Hill (the Majority World), Bernhard Ott (German-speaking Europe), Daniel Aleshire (North America), and Perry Shaw (the Middle East) all point to the combination of theology, skills, and character desired in the formation of leaders.[2]

In the light of this consensus, integration may initially be defined as the process by which Christian theology, practical ministry skills, and godly character are combined and developed in a person for the goal of exercising ministry. This leaves open the issue of who exercises ministry and is formed in this integrated manner; it could be ordained clergy, lay personnel, people serving full-time or part-time, paid or unpaid, those who see their ministry as vocational, or not.

The ICETE statement alerts us to two important dimensions of integration:
1. Integration involves certain content (i.e. theology, skills, and character); and
2. Integration involves a process or processes – what the ICETE statement terms a "holistic *educational approach*." (emphasis added).

These twin issues of the content and process of integration will be prominent in our considerations throughout this book.

Theological education has been grappling with the issue of integration since at least 1950 as it attempts to address the perceived fragmentation of theory and practice.[3] This fragmentation reflects the history of theological education, especially since the Enlightenment.[4] The establishment of the University of Berlin in 1810 set the pattern of practical theology being treated as a discrete area of study from biblical studies, theology, and church history, and was influenced by the twofold approach of *Wissenschaft*, which operated with a critical scientific methodology and sought to train pastors as "professionals,"

---

1. Originally published as "ICETE Manifesto on the Renewal of Evangelical Theological Education."
2. Hill, *Global Church*, 321–26; Ott, *Understanding and Developing*, 199–268; Aleshire, *Earthen Vessels*, 49; Shaw, *Transforming Theological Education*, 3–4.
3. Cahalan, "Integration," 387. See also the important survey in Cheesman, "Competing Paradigms."
4. Farley, *Theologia*, 40–44.

akin to the faculties of law and medicine. The approach of Berlin has profoundly influenced theological education and is regarded as one of the root causes of the fragmentation of theory and practice.[5]

The spread of Western-style theological education with its discrete "fourfold silos" fragmenting theory and practice has created both a problem and an opportunity. The problem is that the separation of head, heart, and hands stands at odds with many cultures found throughout the Majority World. For many of our sisters and brothers who live and minister in collectivist cultures, the fragmentation of theory and practice combined with Western individualism is profoundly unhelpful and also makes no sense. At the same time, this presents an opportunity to learn from theological educators in the Majority World. Those whose first instinct is to integrate all aspects of life and ministry have much to offer. Indeed, as we shall see later in the book, collectivist cultures resonate in important ways with the world of the New Testament in which Paul wrote to Timothy and Titus. In an era of continuing rapid globalization, those of us who serve as theological educators and have the privilege to train and equip women and men for Christian service will benefit from hearing voices from all around the world as we seek to improve theological education.

Challenges for Integration

Despite broad agreement that integration is needed and that it involves combining theology, skills, and character, theological education is faced with two important challenges regarding integration.

1. Lack of Agreement regarding the Process of Integration

In the next chapter we will hear the voices of various theological educators promoting integration. The great positive of this is that there is a huge amount of thought and energy being utilized to improve how theological education is done. However, the variety of approaches highlights the difficulty of the task! Each approach has strengths and weaknesses, and no single approach seems comprehensive enough to achieve all that is desired. And as will become

---

5. Gillham, "Acacia Tree," 111–12.

apparent, there are contradictions and inconsistencies between the various approaches. Theological educators agree that theology, skills, and character should be integrated in the lives of students, but they cannot agree how to do it.

2. Lack of Biblical Reflection on the Topic of Integration

This might seem like an outrageous claim: surely Christian theological educators, and especially evangelical theological educators who have a high view of the authority of Scripture, use the Bible! But it is not as straightforward as that. There is no doubt that the vast bulk of what is published about integration in theological education is written from a Christian worldview. However, very few books and articles discussing integration engage at much depth with the Scriptures. There are some notable exceptions. Robert Banks engages both Old and New Testaments in *Reenvisioning Theological Education*, Bernhard Ott has an extended section in *Understanding and Developing Theological Education*, and Dieumeme Noelliste provides a chapter-length biblical justification for theological education.[6] Others such as Ellen Charry and Daniel Treier reflect *theologically* on theological education but biblical assessments are few and far between.[7]

The lack of biblical reflection upon theological education generally, and integration more particularly, is even more acute when you consider the use of the Letters to Timothy and Titus (hereafter LTT).[8] Even for Banks, the LTT are the focus of only one paragraph and used as supporting references on seven occasions,[9] and Ott confines himself to discussing 2 Timothy 3:16–17.[10]

Why is engaging with the Bible important as we think about integration in theological education? If we accept that the Bible is God's authoritative

---

6. Banks, *Reenvisioning*; Ott, *Understanding and Developing*, 137–98; Noelliste, "Handmaiden."
7. Treier, *Virtue*; Charry, *Renewing*.
8. The letters of 1 and 2 Timothy and Titus have commonly been referred to as the Pastoral Epistles (PE) since the eighteenth century. More recently, this terminology has been regarded as unhelpful because it presupposes the letters should be read together as a "mini corpus" with an ecclesiastical focus. This approach has not given sufficient attention to the character of each letter, nor has it recognized the missionary outlook of the letters. The term "LTT" makes no assumptions about the content of the letters but simply refers to how they are labelled in the New Testament. See Gourgues, *Lettres*, 39–41; Köstenberger, *1–2 Timothy & Titus*, 5–7.
9. Banks, *Reenvisioning*, 121.
10. Ott, *Understanding and Developing*, 165.

word and contains all that is necessary for salvation and godly living, then it must have a voice as we plan how to train people who will be entrusted with the responsibility to teach others of the salvation and godly living centred on Christ and found in the Scriptures. As we critique the content and process of integration, part of that critique must be a biblical critique. As educators, it will not be our only critique: we have other God-given wisdom and resources to draw upon (e.g. educational theories); but as servants of the word entrusted with passing on the good deposit to the next generation, the Bible is a very important voice. Ott says, "what we desperately need, however, are axiomatic biblical-theological principles that can serve as an orientation grid or map for theological education."[11] In addition, Marvin Oxenham believes that, while it is right to be cautious about uncritical, wholesale adoption of biblical forms, it is legitimate to expect to use the Scriptures to support, critique, and offer new insights into educational theories.[12]

In summary, despite broad agreement for the need and content of integration, there is no agreement as to how to facilitate it, and there is a lack of biblical reflection about it.

Why the LTT?

Why use the LTT to have a conversation with theological education about integration?[13]

---

11. Ott, *Understanding and Developing*, 141. Noelliste similarly argues that "Scripture not only corroborates the usefulness of theological learning, but within its ambit, there is sufficient datum for the mounting of a robust apologetic for the very necessity of the enterprise." Noelliste, "Handmaiden," 8.

12. Oxenham, *Character and Virtue*, 163.

13. Given that it is a perennial question in the scholarship of the LTT, the authorship of the LTT needs to be considered regarding how it might influence interaction with the issues of integration in theological education. If we conclude that the apostle Paul did write these letters to real people called Timothy and Titus, then we have an insight into the focus of Paul's training of Timothy and Titus. If we conclude, though, that Paul as writer, and Timothy and Titus as recipients, are fictive (whether through pseudonymity or allonymity), then what we have presented in the LTT is a pattern of Pauline tradition designed for our edification that needs to be taken seriously and learned from. They are still relevant as the most ancient Christian texts we have that deal with the topic of training people for ministry. In addition, each of the letters claims apostolic authority (1 Tim 1:1; 2 Tim 1:1; Titus 1:1–3), giving them a weight equivalent to that of the Old Testament. Whether Paul wrote the LTT or whether they are attributed to him, they

First, while the LTT were not written as a seminary curriculum or as a blueprint for the ideal theological training institution but to leaders of churches,[14] they still have much to offer because they say something about the training of people for ministry.[15]

Second, the LTT discuss topics that intersect with the issue of integration. A quick glance through the contents of commentaries and textbooks dealing with the LTT shows an interest in theology and character, and the themes of leadership, personal example, ethics, mission, education, and godliness are also prominent.[16]

Third, two recent essays suggest that theological education may be awakening to the potential of the LTT to answer its questions about integration. David Starling and Martin Foord both hint at the need for integration and justify it by appealing to the LTT.[17] Starling hints at the need for integration when he calls for the academic, practical, and relational dimensions of ministry formation to have strong biblical and theological foundations in which Christ is central.[18] Similarly, Foord calls for theological education to teach the whole counsel of God found in the Scriptures, to model Christian character, and to develop students' communication and pastoral skills.[19] Both recognize that theology, skills, and character need to be integrated. Strikingly, both writers appeal to the LTT to support their positions. Starling makes use of the steward imagery from Titus 1, with support from both letters to Timothy.[20] Throughout Foord's call for the preparation and training of ministers of the Word for church leadership by the passing on of the gospel tradition and the modelling of

---

must represent the Pauline tradition, or they would not be convincing. Therefore, our study has validity whether one holds to pseudonymous authorship, a neutral position, or authentic Pauline authorship. For ease of reference, throughout the book we refer to Paul, Timothy, and Titus because that is how they are referred to by the LTT themselves.

14. Hamp, "Toward a Pauline Shaping," 15.
15. Hutson, *Timothy and Titus*, 1.
16. E.g. Andria, "1 Timothy, 2 Timothy, Titus"; Towner, *Letters to Timothy and Titus*, 53–62; Matera, *New Testament Theology*, 240–58; Schnelle, *Theology of the New Testament*, 578–601; Köstenberger and Wilder, *Entrusted with the Gospel*.
17. Starling, "The Scribe"; Foord, "Theology of Theological Education."
18. Starling, "The Scribe," 26–27.
19. Foord, "Theology of Theological Education," 37–40.
20. Starling, "The Scribe," 22–23.

godly character, he consistently cites the LTT as the biblical justification for his argument.[21] Starling and Foord are both implicitly calling for integration in theological education and using the LTT to justify their stance. Neither, though, makes any explicit connection between the goal of integration and the LTT. We therefore have the opportunity to engage in this conversation and develop it further.

The Purpose of This Book

This book is a conversation between the theological education sector and the Letters to Timothy and Titus. The chapters that follow have the following aims:
1. To identify what is currently being offered by the theological education sector to promote integration;
2. To hear what the LTT have to say to us about integration;
3. In the light of the above, to develop some principles that might inform the content and practice of integration.

The primary audience I have in mind, therefore, are theological educators and all those around the world who have a stake in theological education, such as pastors, students, mission agencies, and denominational officials. I am using the term "theological education" to refer to the training directed at adults that takes place at a tertiary level of education in a seminary, Bible or theological college, or university.

In the next chapter we will survey the current voices on integration in theological education. In Part B we turn to the LTT. Chapters 3 and 4 examine *what* is integrated in the LTT, and chapter 5 asks *how* this is done. In Part C, chapter 6 looks at current approaches to integration in the light of what we have learned from the LTT, and from this, chapter 7 develops eight principles for theological education. In the final chapter, we attempt to express these eight principles in a working curriculum in both online and face-to-face modes.

My hope is that this book might be a useful resource that stimulates discussion and reflection among theological educators and those stakeholders who share a deep interest in seeing theological education done well to serve

---
21. Foord, "Theology of Theological Education," 34–36.

God's purposes in this world. I have provided some questions at the end of each chapter to help get the conversations started. Perhaps you could work through the book at a faculty retreat or training day, or maybe it could form the basis for discussion at the regular board meeting of your theological education institution.

Discussion Questions

1. Kathleen Cahalan says that integration "is often regarded as the pressing problem of the day" in theological education.[22] Do you agree? Why or why not?

2. Richard and Evelyn Hibbert say that "the key to enhancing theological education is the intentional integration of knowing with being and doing, of theory with practice, and of theology with life and ministry."[23] Do you agree? Why or why not?

3. If you were to survey current students, what would they say are the parts of their training they value the most?

4. What parts of the training would the students say they value the least?

---

22. Cahalan, "Integration," 387.
23. Hibbert and Hibbert, "Better Integration," 107.

2

Current Voices on Integration

Sunil is a gifted evangelist, willing to share the good news of Jesus with people in his part of the city. Encouraged by his pastor, Sunil took some classes through his local seminary to strengthen his grasp of the Bible. But after a year, Sunil gave up studying, saying it was irrelevant and it confused his understanding of the gospel. He just wants to tell people about Jesus.

Shin Shin has loved her time at seminary, delving into theology, exegesis, and church history. And the other students love Shin Shin for her kindness, humility, and willing service. Shortly after leaving seminary, Shin Shin is asked to speak to a group of young women about Jesus. After a week of growing panic, she realizes she does not know how to. She feels deeply ashamed.

Charlie grew up in a good church and as a young man was given opportunities to develop his gift of preaching. Affirmed by his congregation, Charlie went to seminary and added biblical depth to his persuasive preaching style. But whenever anyone criticized Charlie, he was left an emotional wreck.

You may recognize Sunil, Shin Shin, or Charlie. Each of them struggles with integration, even though it shows itself in different ways. Stories such as these are backed up by the statistics. In 2012 Les Ball noted that the common critique by final-year theological students of their study was the "over-intellectual approach to theology and its lack of practical connection to life or ministry."[1] Similarly, in 2013 the Global Survey of Theological Education reported that one of the issues needing most attention is the integration of practical learning

---

1. Ball, *Transforming Theology*, 55.

and academic studies.² Likewise, a major report in 2016 stated that 53 percent of pastors surveyed claimed that seminary did not adequately prepare them for ministry in their faith and skills, despite their being well taught theologically.³

This chapter identifies and describes the contemporary responses of theological educators to the perceived fragmentation of theory and practice. It is important to note that not all these responses understand themselves as models aiming to promote integration. However, each of them wants to renew theological education by breaking down the division between theory and practice. Therefore, while they may or may not use the language of integration, or identify integration as a stated aim, implicitly or explicitly these responses are involved in a conversation about integration. Our task in this chapter is to understand what they are saying.

Previous surveys have tended either to be historical in nature, or to focus on the Athens–Berlin debate spored by Kelsey.⁴ This chapter takes a different approach by bringing together the major proposals of theological educators shaping the conversation about integration.⁵ The survey is organized thematically, with the term "voice" used to refer to a group of proposals coming under a thematic heading:

1. Place Association
2. Missional Theology
3. *Theologia*
4. Wisdom
5. Worship
6. Personal and Spiritual Formation
7. Character Education
8. Reflective Practice
9. Practical Theology
10. Adult Teaching and Learning

---

2. Esterline et al., *Global Survey*, 5.
3. Krejcir, *Statistics on Pastors*, 6.
4. Examples of historical surveys are Farley, *Theologia*, and Ott, *Understanding and Developing*, 15–86. For examples of surveys that begin with the Athens–Berlin discussion, see Das, *Connecting Curriculum with Context*, 41–45; Gillham, "Acacia Tree," 109–12.
5. The closest current attempt is found in Jaison, *Towards Vital Wholeness*, 21–23. Jaison also begins with the Athens–Berlin debate. She lists proposals without going into detail.

11. Curriculum

12. Combinations

Where a proposal straddles the different groupings, it has been classified according to its primary focus. The last group looks at proposals that are combinations drawn from the other eleven.

1. Place Association

Over the last thirty years theological educators have offered several models focusing mainly on what needs to be integrated in theological education. Kelsey's 1993 book *Between Athens and Berlin* characterized theological education as a truce between the personal formation of Christian *paideia* focused on God (Athens) and the critical discipline of theology for the education of clergy (Berlin).[6] In response, Banks proposed a Jerusalem model in which integration occurs as students serve in mission with their trainers.[7] To Kelsey and Banks, Brian Edgar's Geneva model has added the confessional traditions (of whatever flavour) that shape theological education.[8] Darren Cronshaw has incorporated these previous models and adds the dimensions of local and multicultural/multireligious contexts (Auburn and Delhi respectively).[9] Cronshaw argues that the Jerusalem model should be at the centre of this model-matrix because theological education should be organized around mission.[10] More recently, Stephen Haar adapted the work of Banks and Cronshaw to offer a distributed model in which learning takes place through a combination of church, context, and theological education institution settings.[11]

The place association models are helpful at identifying what needs to be integrated. Edgar and Cronshaw's models add contextualization (confessional and missional, respectively) to theology, skills, and character as another key

---

6. Kelsey, *Between Athens and Berlin*, 2–6. *Paideia* can be defined as enculturation through education. Jaeger, *Paideia*, vi; White, *Wise Man*, 29–30. For further discussion see the section, *Revisiting* Paideia *in Theological Education*, in chapter 6.
7. Banks, *Reenvisioning*, 142–43.
8. Edgar, "Theology of Theological Education."
9. Cronshaw, "Reenvisioning Theological Education."
10. Cronshaw, 12.
11. Haar, "Distributed Model."

element requiring integration, but Shaw is critical of the taxonomy of models for being prescriptive and justifying the status quo.[12] Of the models identified, Banks's Jerusalem model offers a process of integration through involvement in mission and reflection upon theology, spirituality, and practical skills in that context, and this has been taken up by Haar to some degree.[13]

In summary, the various place association models of theological education have pinpointed the problem of a lack of integration and have identified that theology, skills, character, and possibly contextualization need integrating.

2. Missional Theology

A second voice treats missional theology as the focal point for theological education. It is a way of doing theology that argues the *missio Dei* is the theological framework for the mission of the church.[14] Given the church is missional by nature and joins in with God's mission, it needs to be led by missional leaders. Therefore, the holistic formation of these leaders should be integrated around missional theology. Bernhard Ott depicts this as shown in Figure 2.1.[15]

The rising influence of the concept of *missio Dei* is usually traced to the 1952 Willingen Conference whose final statement communicated that because God is a missionary, sending his Son and Spirit into the world, the church is missionary by nature.[16] This approach was further promulgated through the influential scholarship of Lesslie Newbigin, David Bosch, and Harvie Conn.[17]

The strength of this approach is its understanding of the relationship between theology and practice. Theology is to shape the practical training of people for leadership in church life. This approach affirms God's plans

---

12. Shaw, "Holistic and Transformative," 208.
13. Banks, *Reenvisioning*, 125–59; Haar, "Distributed Model," 7.
14. Duraisingh, "Ministerial Formation," 33–34; Ott, *Beyond Fragmentation*, 207–11; Guder, "*Missio Dei*," 72; de Gruchy, "Theological Education," 43; Doornenbal, *Crossroads*, 49–54; San, "Contextual Mission Training"; Goheen, "Missional Reading," 304; Kreminski and Frost, "Missional Leadership," 175–86.
15. Ott, *Understanding and Developing*, 191.
16. Goodall, *Missions under the Cross*, 189–90.
17. Newbigin, *Open Secret*; Bosch, *Transforming Mission*; Conn, *Eternal Word*.

centred on Christ for the redemption of the whole creation to his own glory.[18] It also recognizes the context of the post-Christendom world and suggests that theological education needs to train leaders who will think and act as missionaries and will lead local churches in mission. In this sense "missional" is used as an adjective, adding a corrective by highlighting God's mission to the world through his church.[19] Thus missional theology drives the education of leaders for missional practice.

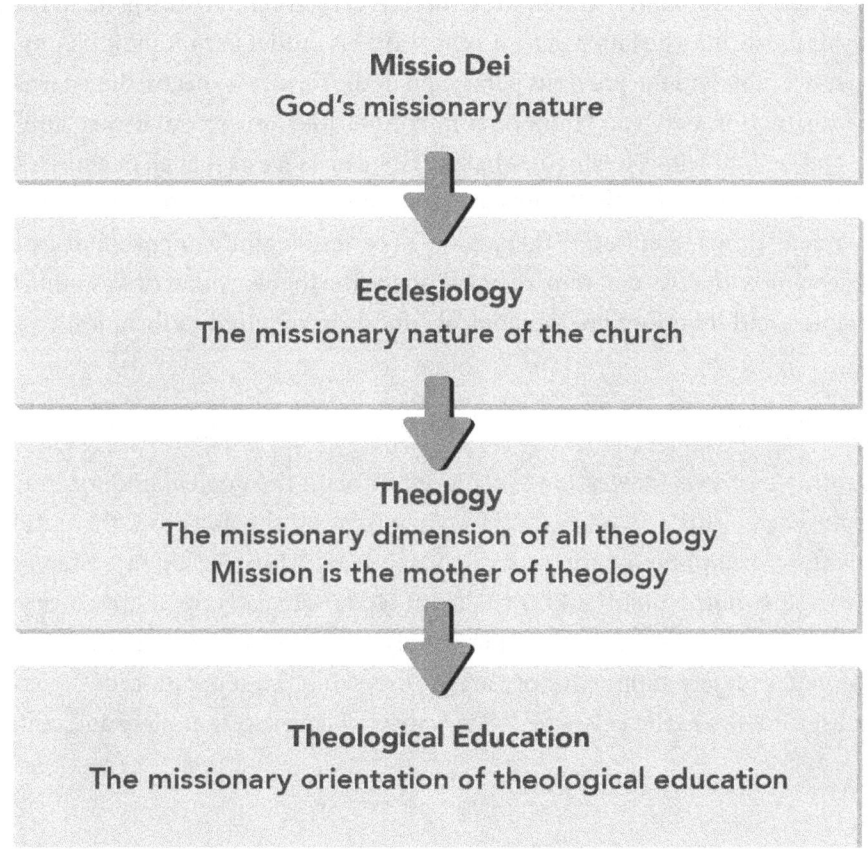

Figure 2.1

---

18. Bauckham, *Bible and Mission*, 11–13; Wright, *Mission of God*, 62–67; Ott and Strauss, *Encountering Theology of Mission*, 55–78.
19. Guder, "Missional Theology," 45; "*Missio Dei*," 65.

Important issues of ecclesiology arise from this approach. The first is whether the church is "missional" in nature or in function.[20] If it is missional by nature, other aspects of its nature (e.g. unity, holiness, universal, apostolic) perhaps should also be included as part of the integrating centre. Second is whether God's church is an agent in the *missio Dei*, or if church (as an expression of the kingdom of God) is a goal of God's mission, or perhaps both. Third, if the church is missionary in its nature, does this mean it is evangelistic by nature, or does it mean that the church is caught up in God's general plans for his creation? The latter fits with the way this model uses "missional" as an adjective, noted in the previous paragraph. If the former is meant, then perhaps the distinction between "missional intention" and "missional dimension" is helpful. In following Newbigin, Michael Goheen suggests that all of church has a missional dimension that points to Christ, and there are specific activities that have a missional intention.[21] These issues of ecclesiology are important because, in keeping with Ott's diagram, they will shape the theology that drives ministry practice, and therefore the theological education required to form leaders.

3. *Theologia*

A third voice says integration is achieved through theological understanding or *theologia*. This approach reacts against treating theology as a theoretical, scientific discipline for the task of church leadership. Farley says *theologia* is the personal, sapiential knowledge of God.[22] He calls for the recovery of *theologia* to counter education that is only academic and pragmatic.[23] Linda Cannell is largely supportive of Farley, perceiving the separation of theology and spirituality as the key issue.[24] She wants to bring together piety and reason

---

20. The theology of God that underpins the understanding of the church as missionary is currently being questioned. Flett affirms that the being and act of God cannot be separated, but Paul questions Bosch's assertion that mission is a divine attribute. Flett, *Witness of God*; Paul, "David Bosch's 'Missio Dei.'"
21. Goheen, "Missional Reading," 314; Newbigin, *One Body*, 21, 43.
22. Farley, *Theologia*, 153, 156.
23. Farley, 151, 194.
24. Cannell, *Theological Education Matters*, 101–2.

in the service of theology.²⁵ For Farley, this reconciliation between *theologia* and scientific theological disciplines occurs in an environment of Christian *paideia* or enculturing, in which there is a dialectic between life and theology.²⁶

Commending this approach is the call to know God personally in a way that shapes a person's character and conduct. *Theologia* identifies that personal character, alongside theology, must be integrated in theological formation and ministry training. In addition, Farley identifies that *theologia* happens through a process of Christian *paideia*.

Three observations are also worth noting. First, *theologia* does not privilege theology but wants it in a dialectical relationship with a personal knowledge of God demonstrated in character. This contrast begins to raise the question as to what relationship theology has with skills and character as they are integrated. Second, *theologia* does not account for the education of people in skills as part of integration. Third, Daniel Treier criticizes Farley for retaining the critical assumptions acceptable in Western universities.²⁷

4. Wisdom

This voice could be regarded as overlapping with *theologia* because of its emphasis on the knowledge of God as transformative for life. This approach builds on *theologia* by using the category of "wisdom" as the focal point of integration. The argument is that wisdom is the appropriate category because it captures the goal of knowing God in a way that produces the best life.²⁸ Wisdom overcomes the division of theory and practice because it combines information and practice that results in *"phronēsis,"* a practical reasoning that knows what to do in various life contexts.²⁹ The process of *paideia* is regarded as a key to the formation of wise people.³⁰ *Paideia* and *phronēsis* are related to each other as process and result. In addition, wisdom as a category has the

---

25. Cannell, "Spiritual Formation," 239.
26. Farley, *Theologia*, 164, 170.
27. Treier, *Virtue*, 19; Farley, *Theologia*, 170–71; Cannell, "Spiritual Formation," 239.
28. Charry, *Renewing of Your Minds*, 234; "Educating for Wisdom."
29. Treier, *Virtue*, 55; Davis and Wadell, "Educating Lives," 94; Vanhoozer, "From Bible to Theology," 243–45; Sayler, "Biblical and Theological Wisdom," 327.
30. Hodgson, *God's Wisdom*, 111–24; Treier, 30; Vanhoozer, 243.

capacity to bring together the Hebrew and Greek backgrounds that influence biblical theology.[31]

The strength of the wisdom approach is its emphasis on knowledge transforming a person who can then navigate life. In this way, wisdom integrates theology, skills, and character. Treier argues that wisdom also has the capacity to integrate mission as a context for learning, and thus can act as the bridge between theology and theological education.[32] As an integrating principle, wisdom shows much promise.

5. Worship

The fifth voice emphasizes that integration occurs through Christian worship. James K. A. Smith argues that people worship what they love, and the cultivation of that love occurs through engaging in various practices.[33] In other words, people become what they do, rather than what they think or believe, which is an emphasis found in other approaches.[34] In addition, worship is a communal activity with God's people providing the context for integration. Worship therefore acts as a bridge between theological education and the church.[35]

This approach takes seriously the call for theological education to address more than the academic part of learning. Like the *theologia* and wisdom approaches, worship involves a personal and experiential knowledge of God, and extends this by offering tangible practices to achieve integration. Through the practice of worship, the knowledge of God is joined with action and expressed through character. Identifying the community of God's people as the context in which the process of integration occurs is also a strength of the worship approach, reflecting the New Testament emphasis of the body of Christ building itself up in love towards maturity in Christ (1 Cor 12–14; Eph 4:1–16). Also worth noting is that the worship approach approximates a form of Christian *paideia* without using the term. Through the practice or habit of

---

31. Hodgson, 125; Treier, 99.
32. Treier, 186–87.
33. Smith, *Desiring the Kingdom*, 46–73.
34. Sayler, "Biblical and Theological Wisdom," 330; Stache, "Formation"; Davis and Wadell, "Educating Lives," 96–98.
35. Stache, "Formation," 290.

worshipping God, people are enculturated to think, act, and love in a certain way in the context of, and for the benefit of, the church and wider society.[36] This continues the theme of *paideia* heard in previous voices.

While the emphasis of the worship approach is on practice, the practices deployed are limited to the personal, relational knowledge of God. Theological educators are also calling for practical skills such as management and preaching to be integrated in the formation of leaders. So, the range of practices in the worship approach may need to be supplemented to achieve integration. In addition, the emphasis on worship as a practice does not sufficiently acknowledge that people have a set of beliefs foundational to their practice. The practice may cultivate what they love, but they must believe something to begin the practice. Like *theologia*, this raises the issue as to how belief (theology) and practice relate to each other.

As with other voices heard so far, the worship approach places an emphasis on a personal and dynamic relationship with God, and takes this further by offering a tangible set of practices for the process of integration.

6. Personal and Spiritual Formation

Another voice promotes personal and spiritual formation as being central to the integration. In keeping with the *theologia*, wisdom, and worship approaches, personal and spiritual formation sees the knowledge of God as personal and experiential. Rather than focusing on a category (e.g. *theologia*, wisdom, worship), this approach is broader in scope and regards formation as the holistic process of a believer growing to maturity in Christ that shows itself in transformed character.[37]

This approach highlights the importance of character formation as part of an integrated theological education. It also seeks to move theology from the academic sphere to the personal domain and connects with skills through the ways they are exercised (e.g. patience and kindness). "Thus spirituality is not

---

36. Smith, *Imagining the Kingdom*, 75–98.
37. Naidoo, "Spiritual Formation," 187; Sands, "What Is Your Orientation?," 15; Harris, "Theological Education," 76–77; Hockridge, "Rethinking Our Approach."

to be understood as yet another discipline to be integrated with the others but rather as an integrative force."[38]

It is also worth noting that there appears to be a degree of congruence between personal and spiritual formation and the concept of *paideia*. Formation is couched as "nurture, direction, discipline, socialization, and inculturation" through reflection and internalizing of the faith – characteristics akin to *paideia*.[39]

Allowing for the strength of the personal and spiritual formation approach, several observations need to be mentioned. First, Robert Brynjolfson asks whether personal and spiritual formation is the most appropriate method for growing skills and academic knowledge.[40] Certainly, formation and the godly character it produces must influence the use of skills, but it may not be the best method to learn and develop the skills themselves. For example, it is desirable for preachers to have godly character, so their messages and lives are consistent. However, preaching is a skill that is developed through practice and feedback over time. Like the worship approach of the previous section, the process of spiritual and personal formation may be too narrow in its focus to integrate the development of skills with theology and character.

Second, the process of personal and spiritual formation can be ill-defined and difficult to measure.[41] Academic knowledge can be measured by assessment pieces, and skills can be demonstrated in front of others, but the criteria on which a person is assessed when it comes to his or her relationship with God and others are not as clear cut. Even a desirable quality such as "authenticity" is difficult to measure unless a substantial amount of time is spent with another person. The result is that it is difficult to measure the degree to which theology, skills, and character have been integrated.

Third, personal and spiritual formation runs the risk of being individualistic. Although mentioning the place of the community of believers, Edward Sands says the primary focus of formation is the growth and development of the

---

38. Ott, *Understanding and Developing*, 208.
39. Ghiloni, "Is Formation Education?," 30; Naidoo, "Spiritual Formation," 191.
40. Brynjolfson, "Missionary Training and Spirituality," 199.
41. Hockridge, "Rethinking Our Approach," 204.

person.⁴² This personal orientation needs to be balanced by connection with Christian community; love for God must be expressed in relating well to others.⁴³

Fourth, it needs to be recognized that students enter theological education already formed to some degree.⁴⁴ Formation is a lifelong process, so students have already been shaped by their own family upbringing, education, church, and work experiences. Those advocating for an integrated theological education must recognize these influences that extend beyond a student's current church or educational context.

The personal and spiritual formation approach emphasizes the importance of godly character and an authentic relationship with God, and is thus in keeping with the approaches of *theologia*, wisdom, and worship. Like the worship approach, it offers practical processes to achieve its goal. Also like the worship approach, the process of personal and spiritual formation may be too narrow to cover all aspects of integration.

7. Character Education

Oxenham distinguishes character education from personal and spiritual formation because of its focus on the growth of settled, virtuous character in the lives of people rather than emphasizing the cultivation of a relationship with God.⁴⁵ This approach argues that character should be central to theological education and integrated with theological knowledge and ministry skills.⁴⁶ This occurs in a learning community in which the goals of character growth are intentionally woven into the curriculum, and thus reflects a *paideia*-style

---

42. Sands, "What Is Your Orientation?," 18.
43. Cole, "A Personalist Perspective," 27.
44. Ghiloni, "Is Formation Education?," 38.
45. Oxenham, *Character and Virtue*, 30–33. However, note the earlier debate between Lindbeck, Tracy, Hall, Smith, and Meye about terminology in their articles in *Theological Education* 24, Supplement 1 (1988). Lindbeck prefers "spiritual formation" to "character formation," Tracy opts for "virtue," Hall argues for "Christian discipleship," Smith says "spiritual formation" and "character formation" are distinct yet related, and Meye wants to join "spirituality" and "character formation." Lindbeck, "Spiritual Formation"; Tracy, "Can Virtue Be Taught?"; Hall, "Character Formation"; Smith, "Spiritual Awareness"; Meye, "Theological Education."
46. Tenelshof, "Character Formation"; Ferdinando, "Character"; Heywood, "Educating Ministers"; Oxenham, *Character and Virtue*, 51, 133–34.

learning.[47] The approach recognizes the difficulty of trying to assess the growth in character in students but is prepared to sit comfortably with the notion that traditional graded assessment pieces are not suited for this purpose.[48]

The character education approach also raises the issue of the relationship between theology, skills, and character in integration. It recognizes that good character is shaped by sound theology, and while not denying the need for skills, character is regarded as more important in order to use the skills.[49] In response to the prominence of knowledge, skills, and spiritual formation, this approach calls for character education to be central to all aspects of theological education, including graduate profiles, curriculum, teaching and learning, and course content and assessment.[50] Although character may stem from good theology, character functions as the most important part of integration.

It is also worth noting that Keith Ferdinando discusses 1 Timothy 4 in support of his argument for the importance of character.[51] However, the discussion also reveals the tension surrounding the place of theology and character as part of integration. He concludes,

> The truth he [the teacher] speaks is to be the truth he lives – in humble submission to God's word, with courage and authority, godliness and diligence. Character is more important than anything else in theological education, for it is vital to the students' own lives and to the task they are being prepared for. And it is the life and words of the teacher – intimately and harmoniously united – that are to make the difference.[52]

Ferdinando clearly regards character as the most important feature of theological education, yet hints that theological truth underpins or is integrated with character, leaving open the question of how they relate together, a question worth investigating in the LTT.

---

47. Tenelshof, 88; Heywood, 16–17; Oxenham, 301–3, 318–25.
48. Oxenham, 357.
49. Ferdinando, "Character," 49–50, 55; Oxenham, 19.
50. Tenelshof, "Character Formation," 88; Oxenham, 132–33.
51. Ferdinando, "Character," 58–63.
52. Ferdinando, 63.

8. Reflective Practice

The next voice says integration in theological education should be centred on the process of reflective practice. Rather than moving from theory to practice (in which theory is privileged), this approach begins with practice.[53] Reflections are made based on experience and then posited as new theoretical knowledge to be tested in further practice. Learning becomes an ongoing cycle of practising theory and theorizing about practice through reflection. Involvement in practice, and stepping back from practice to reflect, are both required.[54] Ott says this paradigm "understands the task of theology as the critical reflection on practice" rather than as theology applied to praxis.[55]

There are several strengths in this approach. First, the process of reflective practice bridges the divide between theory and practice by enforcing a dialogue between the two. Second, learning takes place both in the classroom and in the realm of ministry, thus linking the two contexts. Third, and flowing from the previous points, it overcomes the problem of two (competing) theologies, one drawn from practice and the other academically founded, because theory and practice are mutually informing each other.[56] Fourth, reflective practice has the capacity for integration to go beyond only worship practices or spiritual formation practices to include any form of ministry skill (e.g. sermon preparation and delivery) or situation (e.g. church conflict). Finally, Simon Gilham points out that reflective practice is a process which can be successfully applied in different cultures.[57]

What is ambiguous about reflective practice is the relative authority given to ministry experience or practice and the theory with which it interacts. Gailyn Van Rheenen makes the point that the key issue in contextualization is whether culture or Scripture has priority.[58] In the same sense, the issue must be asked of

---

53. Ott, *Beyond Fragmentation*, 229–34; Paver, *Theological Reflection*, 33–79; Everist and Nessan, "Twelve Pastoral Practices"; Gillham, "Acacia Tree," 115–18; Francis, "Genuinely Reflective Ministry Practitioners"; Hume, "Vision for the Good Life."
54. Ott, 234; Gillham, 116.
55. Ott, 233.
56. Paver, *Theological Reflection*, 4.
57. Gillham, "Acacia Tree," 118.
58. Van Rheenan, "Syncretism and Contextualization," 3–7.

reflective practice: does theory or practice have priority? Is a biblical principle modified in the light of a ministry experience?

The issue of the relative authority given to theory or practice reinforces an earlier question about how theology, skills, and character relate to each other. Like *theologia*, reflective practice employs a dialectical relationship, but it is clearly different from the missional theology in that it relies on practice driving theology, rather than theology driving practice.

Thus, this approach integrates theory and practice with a broad enough capacity to incorporate theology, skills, and character. However, the question as to how these ought to relate together is again highlighted.

9. Practical Theology

Although practical theology is used to describe a curricular area covering subjects such as preaching, pastoral care, evangelism, and leadership, it is as a method of integrating theory and practice in theological education that it is particularly relevant to this survey.[59] Four characteristics are prominent in the practical theology approach. First, it starts with practice before moving to theory and again to practice, a task Richard Osmer says is descriptive, interpretative, normative, and pragmatic.[60] In this sense, it is to be distinguished from applying theology to the practice of ministry; rather, this approach brings the cultural context of life to the fore.[61] Second, practical theology is characterized by reflection and reflexivity signalling a self-conscious involvement on the part of the researcher in the research (e.g. using action research methodology).[62] Third, this approach is multidisciplinary, incorporating insights from fields such as congregational studies, social policy, poetics, liberation theology, and feminist theory.[63] Fourth, theory is not privileged over experience.

---

59. Miller-McLemore, "Contributions of Practical Theology," 5; Cahalan and Nieman, "Mapping the Field."
60. Osmer, *Practical Theology*, 4; Browning, *Fundamental Practical Theology*, 3–9; Espinoza, "Between Text and Context."
61. Woodward and Pattison, "Introduction," 3; Veiling, "On Earth as It Is in Heaven," 161; Major, "Context Is Key."
62. Miller-McLemore, "Practical Theology and Pedagogy," 188; Taylor and Dewerse, "Researching the Future"; Reddie, "Teaching and Researching."
63. Graham, "State of the Art," 174.

The practical theology approach is particularly strong at engaging with the context of real-life situations. By beginning with practice, it helpfully enables theology to be contextualized, and recognizes that all theologizing takes place in a context. In addition, the incorporation of other disciplines provides insights beyond the normal resources of the Christian faith, allowing for a nuanced and sophisticated response to a situation.

However, there are self-identified tensions within practical theology. First, there are calls for a renewed understanding of the relationship between theory and practice.[64] Second, there is disagreement over the place of the Christian tradition (particularly as expressed in the Bible) and the relative authority it carries in the formulation of theology.[65] For example, Terry Veiling says theology cannot claim to present God's narrative for the world and therefore be privileged.[66] On the other hand, Andrew Root makes justification by faith the interpretative grid for understanding practical theology.[67]

10. Adult Teaching and Learning

In the last forty years theological education has made increasing use of adult teaching and learning theories to enhance integration. Rather than simply learning information to be reproduced to pass exams ("surface learning"), integration can be regarded as an example of "deep learning" in which new ideas are analysed, critiqued, and applied by students in real contexts.[68] A variety of approaches have been put forward to achieve this, including transformative learning, andragogy, self-directed learning, dialogue education, authenticity and community, and experiential learning.[69] Within this approach emerge some common features, including a focus on student-centred learning. This

---

64. Miller-McLemore, "Theory–Practice Distinction"; Ward, *Introducing Practical Theology*, 3–4.
65. Ballard, "Use of Scripture"; Graham, "State of the Art," 176–77.
66. Veiling, "'Practical Theology,'" 208–9; "On Earth as It Is in Heaven," 7; Tracy, *Analogical Imagination*, 339.
67. Root, *Christopraxis*. See also the discussion in Ward, *Introducing Practical Theology*, 39–53.
68. Harkness, "Learning Approaches," 143–44.
69. Wickett, "Adult Learning Theories"; Long, "Teaching Adults"; Ball, *Transforming Theology*, especially pp. 11–32; McEwen, "Learning That Transforms"; Heywood, *Kingdom Learning*; Beard, "Adult Learning"; Jaison, *Towards Vital Wholeness*, 153–76.

recognizes that students bring with them a range of experiences from outside theological education which influence and shape their learning. Students are motivated to learn by seeing the applicability of what they are learning to their context and so appreciate a level of autonomy in directing their own learning. It is also important to create an environment that will foster learning, including cultivating strong relationships between learner and teacher, and among other learners. In addition, there is a general pattern to the sequence of learning that begins with the learner's experience, followed by critical reflection, the formulation of new understanding, and the testing of that new understanding in practice.[70]

The application of adult teaching and learning helps theological educators understand how students learn by providing discernible phases as part of a process which (in theory) should improve the capacity for integration. These theories also resonate with the biblical theme of transformation, by seeking to bring change as theology is integrated with a person's character and practice of ministry.[71] As theological educators have sought to apply these theories, there has also been a shift from a generic individualism to an increasing appreciation of the importance of community and context in the learning process which reflects the theological theme of the church living in the world created by God.[72]

However, there are tensions within this approach surrounding the relative authority of experience and theology, and this is manifested in the push to develop new knowledge through critical reflection upon experience as against the desire to pass on the inherited theological tradition.[73] For example, Jack Mezirow's transformative learning approach has been adopted by theological educators, but is critiqued for treating theological knowledge as relative to experience.[74] This tension is an issue already noted in a number of the other approaches to integration.

---

70. For example, see the comparison between Breen & Cockram and Mezirow in Beard, "Adult Learning," 259.
71. McEwen, "Learning That Transforms," 350–54; Beard, 250–52.
72. Fleischer, "Mezirow's Theory," 150–51; McEwen, 350–53; Young, "Transformational Learning," 324.
73. Fleischer, 153; Ball, *Transforming Theology*, 123–25.
74. Melick and Melick, *Teaching That Transforms*, 129–30; Young, "Transformational Learning," 335–36.

11. Curriculum

The eleventh voice says the curriculum of theological education is the tangible expression of the principle of integration. Curriculum is defined as all that happens as part of the theological education institution, including the formal syllabus, activities beyond the classroom, and culture of the institution.[75] Facilitating integration requires the curriculum to be intentional in conception and delivery, including the sequencing of courses so they build on each other, thematic connections between courses, and courses explicitly focusing on integrating what has been studied (e.g. integrative projects).[76] The deliberateness of delivery includes accounting for how students learn and the environments in which learning takes place. The learning environments move beyond listening in a classroom to include interactive learning and participation in a ministry context.[77] Without such intentional curriculum design and delivery, an in-principle commitment to integration is undermined.

Integration through curriculum raises the issue as to what the content of the curriculum is, and how its various components relate together. The theological education sector is in broad agreement that the content of its curriculum should include theology, skills, and character, but within that mix, biblical and theological training is regarded as primary.[78] Goheen nuances this to make the "missionary encounter between the gospel and the cultural story" as the most important part of the curriculum, which reflects a combination of the first two of Ball's governing principles (biblical primacy, and theology engaging culture and society).[79] While curriculum design sees the development of godly character and acquisition of skills as essential, biblical and theological knowledge is regarded as primary, thus setting up a potential clash of priorities in curriculum design and delivery. Once again, as has been observed across the various approaches, the question of how theology, skills, and character relate to one another comes to the fore.

---

75. Jaison, *Towards Vital Wholeness*, 35–37; Shaw, *Transforming Theological Education*, 51–119.
76. Gaikward, "Curriculum Development"; Shaw, 4–5; Ball, *Transforming Theology*, 126; Ott, *Beyond Fragmentation*, 240; Cahalan, "Integration," 389–91.
77. Harkness, "De-Schooling the Theological Seminary," 146, 152; Banks, "Paul as Theological Educator"; Goheen, "Missional Reading," 325–26.
78. Ball, *Transforming Theology*, 124; Ott, *Understanding and Developing*, 184.
79. Goheen, "Missional Reading," 312; Ball, 125.

12. Combinations

As has been hinted at through this survey, there are a range of proposals that use combinations of the eleven approaches identified to integrate theology, skills, and character. Curriculum is the most common partner for other approaches, which is not surprising given that the issues have arisen in, and are being addressed by, the theological education sector. There is no noticeable pattern in which approaches are used together. For example, curriculum is combined with missional theology (Goheen, Shaw), *theologia* (Cannell), and personal and spiritual formation (Marilyn Naidoo, Diane Hockridge). Worship is joined with missional theology (Kristine Stache) or wisdom (Gwen Sayler, Darin Davis and Paul Wadell), while Cronshaw seeks to express his approach through personal and spiritual formation. Reflective practice is combined with missional theology (Christopher Duraisingh, Steve de Gruchy), and is also brought together with the Jerusalem model and curriculum by Banks. Personal and spiritual formation is combined with missional theology and curriculum (Karina Kreminski and Michael Frost), and Oxenham teams character education with curriculum and reflective practice. Perhaps the most comprehensive combination of approaches can be found in the proposals of Ott and Jessy Jaison. Ott's work accounts for the models previously proposed, builds from a foundation of missional theology, and incorporates reflective practice and spiritual formation in an intentionally designed curriculum involving the contexts of both church and academy. Similarly, Jaison draws from previous models, calls for God's word to underpin theological education, and wants spiritual formation, adult learning, and curriculum and assessment to collaborate as the academy serves the church. In summary, the combination approach indicates the strong desire for integration in theological education and the difficulty in achieving it.

Observations

Our survey identifies a broad spectrum of voices calling for integration in theological education, ranging in emphasis from the theoretical and theological to the personal and pragmatic. What observations can we make?

First, *most educators see integration flowing from a presupposition of personal, relational faith; knowledge ought not to be only cognitive and academic.*

The approaches of *theologia*, wisdom, worship, and personal and spiritual formation emphasize that cognitive knowledge about God must translate into an affective relationship with God that will show itself in the character of the person as he or she grows in Christlike maturity. Therefore, a significant part of integrated formation is a personal, relational knowledge of God.

The theme of the relational knowledge of God may be regarded as part of a reaction against the Berlin model and its treatment of theology as a science with critical presuppositions. Those seeking greater integration do not dismiss the rigour of critical enquiry but want to move the starting point from one of suspicion to one of personal, relational faith. This provides the motivation for the integration of theology, skills, and character, and facilitates its process. With a presupposition of personal, relational faith, a theological insight carries with it both indicative and imperative; a truth revealed through study needs to be integrated in a person's character and lived out.

Second, *there are tensions in the understanding of how theology, skills, and character relate together*. The missional theology and curriculum approaches regard theology as primary, character education names theology as foundational but functions with character as central, the worship approach marginalizes theology in favour of practice, while the *theologia*, reflective practice, and practical theology approaches embrace theology in a dialectical relationship. These contradictory observations point to the need for greater clarity as to how theology, character, and skills ought to relate to one another.

The need to investigate this relationship is further suggested by the functionality of some of the approaches. Some function as frameworks for the process of integration; integration happens at the theoretical level providing the umbrella under which to incorporate theology, skills, and character. The *theologia*, missional theology, and wisdom proposals each work this way. And although the place association approach is used diagnostically, it too provides a theoretical framework for integration.

This raises other important issues, including whether integration requires an overarching framework or not. The *theologia*, missional theology, and wisdom approaches each argue for a theological framework but differ in their particularities. This suggests that theology is primary even if character and skills are essential. There are, however, enough alternatives to signal that this position should be tested. Cronshaw places Banks's Jerusalem model at the centre of theological education arguing that mission is the focal point of integration. In other words, missional practice rather than theology is primary and therefore acts as the framework. An alternative could be that theology, skills, and character are much more mutually interdependent, without one claiming primacy.

The issue of context in a range of approaches adds further weight to the need to investigate the relationship between theology, skills, and character. The nature of the relationship between content (theory or theology) and context (experience or practice) is ambiguous about which has primary authority, and this is exemplified in the practical theology, reflective practice, and curriculum approaches. It also intersects with ecclesiology at two levels, within both the church context, and the context of the church's interaction with the wider culture. Within the context of the church itself, does theology or context have primacy? Similarly, does theology or culture have primacy in the interaction between church and the wider society? How theology relates to context has a bearing on the functional authority of theology within an integrated theological education.

The tension between different models, the function of some of the approaches as frameworks, and the issue of context combine to highlight that central to the topic of integration is the issue of the relationship between theology, skills, and character. The primacy of theology and its function as a framework for integration need to be tested.

Third, *there is no agreement regarding the process of integration*. Worship, personal and spiritual formation, reflective practice, practical theology, and curriculum are all examples of approaches seeking to integrate theory and practice. This suggests that no one process may be appropriate to fully integrate theology, skills, and character. A range of processes and activities may be needed depending on what is being learned; a formal lecture may suit learning a set of cognitive facts, while an informal conversation may suit character development. The formal and informal curriculum needs to reflect the range of contexts and processes and the contribution each makes to integration.

Coupled with this is the emergence of the theme of *paideia* evident in several approaches, either by name or by concept. In reaction against a "knowledge dump" and the difficulty of translating theory into practice, *paideia* is regarded as a process that may facilitate integration.

Conclusion

An enormous amount of thought and energy is being expended grappling with the issue of integration, and this is to be applauded. However, our survey of the current voices in theological education has identified that

1. *most educators see integration flowing from a presupposition of personal, relational faith;*
2. *there are tensions in the understanding of how theology, skills, and character relate together; and*
3. *there is no agreement regarding the process of integration.*

Given these tensions, the aim of the next few chapters is to examine the LTT to see what insights they might offer.

Discussion Questions

1. Describe what integration looks like in your context.

2. What are the strengths and weaknesses of the approach you are using to achieve integration?

3. In your context, which is regarded as more important: theology, skills, or character?

4. Who could you speak with to find out more about facilitating integration?

Part B

Integration in the Letters to Timothy & Titus

3

What Is Integrated in 1 Timothy?

What qualities were valued in potential leaders as you were growing up? What were they looking for in the local church that shaped you, and the broader Christian community you were a part of? Where did the *emphasis* fall? If you had to rank theology, skills, and character in order of importance, what were the messages you received? Were there other qualities that were also valued?

All of us are, to a degree, products of our upbringing, including the formative influence of our Christian subculture. This means we bring our presuppositions and preferences to any discussion, including a discussion about integration. It is good to be honest with ourselves about where we have come from, and our current stance, so that we might exercise a posture of humility as we listen to each other, and to God's word.

What can we learn from the LTT about integration? In this and the following chapter we will look for evidence of *what* is integrated, and we will discover that not only are theology, skills, and character integrated in the LTT, but they also integrate identity, ministry, and suffering. We will also consider how integration might fit within the purposes of each letter.[1]

---

1. I have argued elsewhere that the concept of integration was part of the Jewish and Graeco-Roman worlds, and Paul has filled it with fresh Christian content. See Wright, "'Integration' in the Ancient World."

Focus Passage: 1 Timothy 4:6–16

> ⁶ If you put these instructions before the brothers and sisters, you will be a good servant of Christ Jesus, nourished on the words of the faith and of the sound teaching that you have followed. ⁷ Have nothing to do with profane myths and old wives' tales. Train yourself in godliness, ⁸ for, while physical training is of some value, godliness is valuable in every way, holding promise for both the present life and the life to come. ⁹ The saying is sure and worthy of full acceptance. ¹⁰ For to this end we toil and struggle, because we have our hope set on the living God, who is the Saviour of all people, especially of those who believe.
>
> ¹¹ These are the things you must insist on and teach. ¹² Let no one despise your youth, but set the believers an example in speech and conduct, in love, in faith, in purity. ¹³ Until I arrive, give attention to the public reading of scripture, to exhorting, to teaching. ¹⁴ Do not neglect the gift that is in you, which was given to you through prophecy with the laying on of hands by the council of elders. ¹⁵ Put these things into practice, devote yourself to them, so that all may see your progress. ¹⁶ Pay close attention to yourself and to your teaching; continue in these things, for in doing this you will save both yourself and your hearers.

First Timothy 4:6–16 provides evidence that theology, skills, and character are to be integrated in the life of Timothy, with verses 7 to 15 elaborating on the summary statements that frame the section (vv. 6, 16). Paul encourages Timothy to be a "good servant of Christ Jesus" (καλὸς ἔσῃ διάκονος Χριστοῦ Ἰησοῦ, v. 6). Combining the adjective "good" with ministry or service is consistent with the descriptions of the overseers and deacons in chapter 3 (see following section) and indicates that Timothy is to be highly competent at what he does.[2] Underpinning Timothy's competency is the sound teaching of the gospel that he has continued to train himself (ἐντρεφόμενος) in, and he is to teach the same to the congregation.[3] This teaching task (ὑποτιθέμενος) is

---

2. Perkins, *Pastoral Letters*, 83.
3. Smith, *Pauline Communities*, 323.

usually translated as to "put before" (NRSV, ESV) or to "point out" (NIV, NASB, HCSB), but given the context of 4:1–5 and the threat of false teaching, the task carries authority.[4] Timothy is to exercise skilful ministry for the benefit of the church by teaching them the truth of the gospel, a truth that shapes his own life.

Verses 7 to 15 expand upon this. Timothy is to train himself to be godly (v. 7) and set an example to other believers as to what godliness looks like by the way he talks, acts, loves, and is faithful and pure (v. 12). The *gar* (γὰρ) of verse 8 indicates the theological reason for pursuing godly behaviour: godliness promises life now and in the coming age.

Godly character is to be combined with sound theology. Timothy is to turn away from false teaching (v. 7) and instead continue in the "words of the faith and of the sound teaching that you have followed" (v. 6).[5] This is paralleled by "the teaching" (τῇ διδασκαλίᾳ) in verse 16 which helps frame the section. In keeping with verses 8 and 10, the offer of salvation in verse 16 is tied up with truthful teaching, and contrasts the healthy content and effects of Timothy's teaching with that of the opponents and their followers (vv. 1–2).

Alongside godly character and sound theology, verse 14 points to a gift or ability (τοῦ . . . χαρίσματος) given by God that Timothy is aware of and that is to be used.[6] The exact details of Timothy's gift are not specified, though Blight lists a number of suggestions including preaching and teaching, discerning true and false teaching, and leadership; Krause adds prophecy, and Fiore the spirit of love, power, and self-control.[7] Two clues in the immediate context may help. First, Timothy must "command [Παράγγελλε] and teach [δίδασκε] these things" (v. 11), with both being imperatives. This points to the leadership and teaching Timothy is to exercise among the congregation. The second clue reinforces this. The definite articles of verse 13 show that the public reading of Scripture, preaching, and teaching are activities central to the public gathering of the congregation and Timothy is to exercise his gifts of leadership and teaching when the church meets together.

---

4. Oberlinner, *Die Pastoralbriefe*, 1.188; Knight, *Pastoral Epistles*, 193.
5. Mutschler argues that v. 6 is the only example in the letter of "the faith" referring to the objective content of orthodoxy and teaching. Verses 1–2 would suggest otherwise. Mutschler, *Glaube in den Pastoralbriefen*, 392–93.
6. Knight, *Pastoral Epistles*, 208; Quinn and Wacker, *Letters to Timothy*, 391.
7. Blight, *Exegetical Summary*, 259; Krause, *1 Timothy*, 93; Fiore, *Pastoral Epistles*, 96.

The broader context of the letter also supports the idea that Timothy's gifts were leadership and teaching. The vocabulary of *parangellō* (παράγγελλω) is also used to frame the letter and express the leadership Timothy is to exercise (1:3, 18; 6:17), including directing the congregation's care for widows (5:7). Timothy is also to "teach and exhort these things" (Ταῦτα δίδασκε καὶ παρακάλει, 6:2). The themes of exercising authoritative leadership and teaching are threaded through the letter and support the idea from 4:11–16 that these are the gifts with which God has endowed Timothy.

The passage closes with a summary exhortation: Timothy is to "pay close attention to [him]self and to [the] teaching" (v. 16). Timothy is to keep growing in godliness as outlined in verse 12 and hold to sound doctrine. Personal character and the content and skill of teaching are all to receive Timothy's vigilant ongoing scrutiny, highlighting that this role and its tasks should not be compartmentalized from who he is as a person. Thus, 1 Timothy 4:6–16 displays clear evidence that theology, skills, and character were to be integrated in the life of Timothy as he exercised ministry.

1 Timothy 6:11–16

The integration of identity, godly character, and theology is also observable in 1 Timothy 6:11–16. Timothy's identity as a "man of God" links him to Old Testament figures such as Moses (Deut 33:1), Elijah (1 Kgs 17:18), and David (2 Chr 8:14), and points to his role as a speaker of God's word.[8] Rather than be caught up in the love of money (6:10), Timothy is to pursue godly character and living (v. 11), and fighting the good fight of faith indicates holding on to the truth of the gospel. Paul's charge to Timothy is given great weight as Paul calls God and Christ Jesus as witnesses (v. 13), so Timothy is to keep the command (τὴν ἐντολήν) without spot or blemish (v. 14). While the "command" could refer to the exhortations of verses 11 and 12, given that it is a single commandment it is more likely to be an all-encompassing reference to what Paul has instructed Timothy in the letter.[9] This would also be in keeping with Paul's purpose in writing (3:14–15). Consistent with his identity as a "man of

---

8. Krause, 128; Collins, *Timothy and Titus*, 162.
9. Dibelius and Conzelmann, *Pastoral Epistles*, 89; Yarbrough, *Timothy and Titus*, 328.

God," Timothy is to hold to what is true and live a godly life in the knowledge that the Lord Jesus will return. Perseverance in faithfulness to the truth and godly character are theologically motivated.

The evidence suggests that as a "man of God," Timothy is to hold to the truth, live a godly life, and use his gifts of leading and teaching for the benefit of believers, so they enjoy salvation now and for ever. The integration of identity, theology, skills, character, and ministry are found in Timothy.

Overseers and Deacons

Evidence of the integration of theology, skills, and character is also found in the overseers and deacons of 1 Timothy 3:1–13. The importance of congregational oversight is emphasized by its designation as a trustworthy saying (1 Tim 3:1).[10] Verses 1 and 2 are linked by "it is therefore necessary" (δεῖ οὖν), indicating that the first qualification for an overseer is character that is above reproach (ἀνεπίλημπτον), with verses 2 and 3 filling out what this looks like in practice. Verse 7 indicates that it is necessary that the overseer's reputation for good character extends beyond the congregation and is known among the wider unbelieving community. The reputation of the elders is also important within the congregation; while groundless rumours are to be ignored, elders are not beyond scrutiny for their sin, providing there is evidence to support such claims (5:19– 20).[11]

In addition to blameless character, the overseer must be apt to teach (διδακτικόν, v. 2). If the overseers in 3:1–7 are the same group as the elders in 5:17, then those who work at preaching and teaching (λόγῳ καὶ διδασκαλίᾳ) are worthy of honour among the congregation, including financial support. Another skill required of overseers is the ability to lead and manage people

---

10. Scholarship is divided as to whether the "faithful saying" refers to what comes before (2:15) or after it (3:1b). For arguments, see Mounce, *Pastoral Epistles*, 167. Swinson argues that the faithful sayings are a more general reference to the apostolic gospel, but in practice links 1 Tim 3:1a to the content of 1 Tim 2:15. See Swinson, "Πιστὸς Ὁ Λόγος," Campbell says 1 Tim 3:1a refers to 1 Tim 3:16. Campbell, "Identifying the Faithful Sayings," 81. What is not discussed is the context of the chapter, which shows that God's church is to protect and promote the truth of God's plan of salvation, providing the reason why the faithful saying should be linked to verse 1b.
11. The terms πρεσβύτερος and ἐπίσκοπος refer to the same role. See Merkle, *Elder and Overseer*, 148–57; H. W. Beyer, "ἐπίσκοπος," *TDNT*, 2.617.

very well (3:3–4; 5:17).¹² The word *proistēmi* (προϊστημι) conveys the twin ideas of to lead and to care.¹³ Oversight involves the skilful leading and directing of, and caring for, God's people, with the use of *kalōs* (καλῶς) in both 3:4 and 5:17 emphasizing the high degree of competency required.¹⁴ Evidence of *proistēmi* must first be observable in the households of any potential overseers before they are given responsibility for oversight of the congregation (3:4–5).

What is not explicit in 3:1–7 is the place of theology in the lives of the overseers, though this is implied by the wider context of chapter 3. God's church is to protect and promote the truth of his plan of salvation (3:15).¹⁵ The overseers are to ensure God's church fulfils its task as the pillar and bulwark of the truth, through their teaching and the leadership and care of the congregation in the face of false teaching.¹⁶ The context suggests that the content of their teaching is the truth which is the mystery of godliness (3:16).

Like the overseers, deacons are to be above reproach (ἀνέγκλητοι, 3:10), with 3:8, 12 highlighting their trustworthy speech, lack of drunkenness or greed, and faithfulness in marriage. Whether 3:11 is taken to refer to female deacons or the wives of male deacons, the point is the same: they must be of good character.¹⁷

Also like the overseers, the deacons must display the skill of leading and managing people in their own household (προϊστάμενοι, 3:12). However, no reference is made to their teaching ability, suggesting this was the domain

---

12. Oberlinner, *Die Pastoralbriefe*, 1.115, says the passage emphasizes management ability and marginalizes teaching ability. This is difficult to sustain in the broader context of the letter with its emphasis on teaching sound doctrine.

13. B. Reicke, "προϊστημι," *TDNT*, 6.701.

14. Malherbe, "Overseers as Household Managers," 78–80, sees the emphasis falling on administration rather than leading.

15. Spicq ties together salvation and ecclesiology. While acknowledging that salvation comes through Christ, he says that because the church is the pillar of the truth, those outside the church are outside salvation. However, while it is right to say that a believer does not enjoy salvation through the truth of Christ without being brought into the church, this view does not account for the opponents who have abandoned the truth (1 Tim 4:1) but are still part of the church. Spicq, *Les Épîtres pastorales*, 1.258.

16. Brox, *Die Pastoralbriefe*, 157.

17. For discussion of the options, see Marshall, *Pastoral Epistles*, 492–95; Köstenberger, *1–2 Timothy & Titus*, 133–34.

of the overseers.[18] There is a common expectation that both overseers and deacons will be highly proficient at their roles, with the adverb "well" (καλῶς) occurring in the letter in connection with their ministries (3:4, 12, 13; 5:17).[19]

Unlike the elders, though, direct reference is made to the theology of the deacons. "They must hold fast to the mystery of the faith with a clear conscience" (3:9). This anticipates the term "the mystery of godliness" (ESV; τὸ τῆς εὐσεβείας μυστήριον) in verse 16 which provides the content of the mystery and focuses on the historical events of Jesus Christ. "Mystery" is a term of revelation, which is in keeping with its usage in Colossians and Ephesians where it refers to "the eschatological fulfilment of God's plan of salvation in Christ."[20] The passive *ephanerōthē* (ἐφανερώθη) of verse 16 indicates Christ's incarnation was God's initiative to bring salvation.[21] The humanity of his life is emphasized, and implicit in his being raised to life is his death. The news of his resurrection is now preached among the nations in keeping with the promises to Abraham, so that all may come to faith. Line 6 (Christ being taken up in glory) parallels line 3 (Christ being seen by angels) and refers to Christ's exaltation or enthronement in heaven.[22] Verse 15 uses "the truth" to parallel "the mystery of godliness." In holding to the mystery of the faith, the deacons are standing firm on the truth that is grounded in the historical events of Christ.[23]

The overseers and deacons are to be above reproach, demonstrating godly character. The deacons are to hold to the truth or mystery of the faith, and the broader context of chapter 3 suggests the overseers must do the same. Both groups must show very good skills in managing and leading people, and in addition, the overseers must be apt to teach. The evidence points to

---

18. Roloff, *Der erste Brief an Timotheus*, 164, says the overseers are drawn from the ranks of the previously tested deacons. Similarly, in arguing that deacons are apprentice overseers, Patrick says teaching may be the defining mark of the overseers. See Patrick, "Pastoral Offices," 167.

19. Yarbrough, *Timothy and Titus*, 214; Towner, *Letters to Timothy and Titus*, 255.

20. O'Brien, *Ephesians*, 110. See Eph 1:9; 3:3–4, 9; 5:32; 6:19; Col 1:27; Knight, *Pastoral Epistles*, 182, says "mystery" is a "term of revelation."

21. Martin, "1 Timothy 3:16," 111.

22. Akin, "Mystery of Godliness," 140.

23. Hentschel, *Diakonia im Neuen Testament*, 400.

the necessity of the integration of theology, skills, and character in the lives of the overseers and deacons.

Paul

Theology, skills, character, ministry, and identity are integrated in the life of Paul, and can be found in 1 Timothy 1:11–20; 2:3–7; 4:10; and 6:6–8. His role as an apostle comes at the command of God with the hope of Christ Jesus as a theological mooring (1:1). Paul regards himself as the prime example of the foremost sinner who has received the superabundant grace, mercy, and love of Christ Jesus (1:14–16).[24] The grace that now defines him has also brought about a change in his character. In his former life (τὸ πρότερον, v. 13) Paul was an ignorant and unbelieving "blasphemer and a persecutor and a violent man" (1:13–14), but now he endorses righteousness, godliness, faith, love, endurance, and gentleness (6:11). The change of identity and character has also brought with it a change of role and activity. God has now entrusted the gospel to Paul, and the Lord Jesus has appointed him to his service, empowering Paul for the ministry (1:11–12). Paul regards the change of identity, character, and role in his life as all to the praise and glory of God (1:17). Theology also drives Paul's ministry practice in his treatment of Hymenaeus and Alexander who have shipwrecked their faith (1:18–20). In response, Paul has delivered them over to Satan, which in the light of 1 Corinthians 5:5 suggests that they are to be treated as unbelievers with the view to them repenting and turning to Christ.[25] Paul wants them to be educated or to learn (παιδευθῶσι, v. 20) not to blaspheme. Just as Paul, a blasphemer who acted in ignorance and unbelief (1:13), was shown mercy, he also wants Hymenaeus and Alexander to turn from their distortion of the truth and receive God's grace. Paul's practice of church discipline reflects his theology.

Similar themes are present in 1 Timothy 2:3–7. In 2:7 he describes himself as a preacher and apostle, with the focus of his ministry being as a "teacher of the Gentiles in faith and truth." This places Paul's ministry in line with God's promises to Abraham to bless the nations and Jesus's commission to make

---

24. The use of εἰμὶ ἐγώ in 1:15 emphasizes Paul's self-understanding.
25. Fiore, *Pastoral Epistles*, 12, 54; Saarinen, *Pastoral Epistles*, 47–48.

disciples of all nations (Gen 12:3; Matt 28:18–20). The content of that truth is God's saving plan through the ransom of Christ's death, captured in 2:3–6. "For this" (εἰς ὅ, 2:7) links Paul's purpose and identity with God's saving purposes in Christ for the nations. Who Paul is and what he does is an outworking of his theological understanding of God's plans. Coupled with this, Paul's self-designation as a "teacher" implies his skill in the task. Those who bore the title of teacher in the ancient world were expected to be competent at instructing others, suggesting that as well as providing truthful content, Paul is very good at how he teaches.[26] This stands in contrast to the teachers who teach false doctrine and lack skill in teaching (1 Tim 1:3, 7–8).

Paul's ministry is hard work; he and Timothy labour and strive (4:10). Verse 10 is linked to what comes both before and after it, demonstrating the purpose and reason for the hard work of ministry. "For to this" (εἰς τοῦτο γὰρ) links the purpose of labouring and striving to the faithful saying of verse 8.[27] The purpose of working hard in ministry is so other people will experience and grow in godliness that offers life now and in the future. This is not a task done in vain, with the *hoti* (ὅτι) of verse 10 pointing to the reason why: Paul and Timothy's hope is "set on the living God, who is the Saviour of all people, especially of those who believe." The labouring and toiling in ministry is given theological purpose and reason, pointing to the integration of theology and ministry practice.

Paul also includes himself in the discussion of contentment in chapter 6. In contrast to the false teachers who think godliness is a means to financial gain (v. 5), "there is great gain in godliness combined with contentment" (v. 6), with material contentment defined in terms of having food and clothing (v. 8).[28] These verses reinforce that godly character is important to Paul and that one of its tangible expressions is a simple lifestyle content with God's provision.

First Timothy suggests that Paul's understanding of God as the living saviour and provider, and of his rescue plan for the world centred on Christ, are integrated with Paul's identity, character, purpose, and skilful practice of

---

26. Bonner, *Education in Ancient Rome*, 20–27; John 3:1–10.
27. While there is discussion as to what πιστὸς ὁ λόγος (v. 9) refers to, the majority of scholars opt for some or all of v. 8, based on the γὰρ of v. 8 introducing the saying. For a survey of the discussion see Mounce, *Pastoral Epistles*, 247–48; Marshall, *Pastoral Epistles*, 554.
28. Shelter may also be in view. See Malherbe, "Godliness, Self-Sufficiency," 395.

ministry. This is relevant because whether Paul is the real author or only the named author, it represents the Pauline tradition.

The Church

The overseers and deacons are drawn from the wider church, so it should be expected that there would be a level of consonance regarding what was required of them. What we discover is that there is evidence of the integration of theology and behaviour in the life of the church, and so it acts as a normal expectation for all believers.

In 1 Timothy 1:5, Timothy is to command those teaching false doctrine to stop (1:3); "the aim of such instruction is love that comes from a pure heart, a good conscience, and sincere faith" (v. 5). Towner argues this trio points to the connection of true belief, inner transformation, and tangible action.[29] Love in the church will be the manifestation of true and living faith, and evidence of the integration of internal convictions and outward behaviour.

In 1 Timothy 2:1–15, the theology is contained in verses 3–6 and speaks of God's desire and plan to save people through the ransoming death of Jesus. Based on this theological indicative, the church is to pray for all people (v. 1), reflecting God's desire to save all people (v. 4).[30] Prayers are for those in authority with the expectation of peace, providing conditions for living godly lives and the spread of God's saving message. Believing men everywhere are urged to pray without anger and disputes (v. 8), with the manner of their prayers to reflect holiness. Likewise, the women who are skilful at worshipping God are to demonstrate this with their good deeds, modesty, and decency, rather than ostentatious displays of wealth (vv. 9–10).[31] Thus the good ordering of the gathered church is grounded theologically.

The ordering of the church is also discussed in 1 Timothy 3:14–16. Paul wants Timothy to know the behaviour necessary among the congregation that comes with their identity as God's household, his church, the pillar and

---

29. Towner, *Goal of Our Instruction*, 154–59.
30. Roloff, *Der erste Brief an Timotheus*, 15, 119.
31. Yarbrough, *Timothy and Titus*, 168.

foundation of the truth.³² The historical foundation of the truth is "the mystery of godliness" (τὸ τῆς εὐσεβείας μυστήριον) which is outlined in verse 16 and describes the events of Christ's incarnation, resurrection, glorification, and proclamation throughout the world. In other words, because of the church's identity and function in holding up and holding out the truth, there are implications for their conduct.³³ Timothy is to know this, help the congregation live in line with it, and, by implication, live in line with it himself. These verses point to the integration of theology and godly behaviour for Timothy and the church.

Some of the clearest indications of the integration of belief and behaviour in congregational life are found in 5:1–6:2 which is structured around the references to "honour" older and younger men and women, widows, elders, and masters. It is to be a priority (πρῶτον) for families to learn to practise godliness (εὐσεβεῖν) by caring for their own widows (5:4).³⁴ The theological underpinning of this is that it pleases God. Negatively, failure to provide for widows in his or her own family means someone "has denied the faith and is worse than an unbeliever" (v. 8). Just as right theology is to drive right behaviour, so too poor theology drives inappropriate behaviour.

Paul's call for younger widows to remarry reaffirms God as the good creator. The false teachers were forbidding people to marry (4:3). If the young widows were influenced by the false teachers, they might be caught between the teaching not to marry and their desire to remarry.³⁵ In order to remarry, they would violate their first pledge and abandon the faith. The phrase *tēn prōtēn pistin* (τὴν πρώτην πίστιν, 5:12) is generally translated as "pledge."³⁶ However, 5:4 uses *prōtēn* to indicate the sense of priority children should have in the care of widows. Similarly, the use of *prōtēn* in 2:1 indicates the theological priorities Paul wants to address.³⁷ This would suggest that 5:12 should be understood as "the first faith": in other words, the faith is of first importance or priority. This

---

32. Gourgues, *Lettres*, 135–37, argues that Timothy is the pillar and foundation of the truth. However, the syntax suggests the pillar and foundation most naturally refer to the church.
33. Akin, "Mystery of Godliness," 140.
34. Barclay, "Household Networks," 270–76.
35. Fee, *1 & 2 Timothy, Titus*, 114–15, 121.
36. E.g. NIV, NRSV, NASB. The ESV and NKJV translate it as "faith."
37. Gibson, "Literary Coherence," 65.

is supported by the grave concern Paul expresses in 5:15 that some widows have already turned away (ἐξετράπησαν) to follow Satan.[38] Paul's solution is to affirm the place of remarriage (v. 14), reinforcing God's good creation purposes (4:1–5); the behavioural solution is underpinned by correct theology.

Paul's concern for right theology to be expressed in right behaviour also has a missionary concern. In the Graeco-Roman world, those with the charge of the dowry had legal responsibility for the care of a widow.[39] Any failure of believers to care for widows in their households was to do less than was required and expected by the surrounding society, and would bring the gospel into disrepute in the eyes of those outside the church. Similarly, Paul realizes that younger widows turning from the faith provides the watching world with an opportunity to slander God and his people (v. 14). In 6:1–2, Christian slaves are called on to honour their masters, whether they are Christian (v. 2) or not (v. 1). The *hina* (ἵνα) of verse 1 indicates the purpose of this behaviour – that God's name and the teaching would not be slandered – and reflects the LXX of Isaiah 52:5. In short, 5:1–6:2 shows that there are behavioural implications that flow from wanting to please God, as well as demonstrating a clear concern for the standing of the Christian message in the community.

First Timothy demonstrates that the character and behaviour of believers in the church is integrated with theology, and that it is exemplified in *eusebeia*. As such, a well-functioning church produces people who are eligible to act as overseers and deacons because of their sound doctrine and godly living.

Signs of the Wrong Type of Integration

There is also evidence in the letter of the wrong type of integration. The opening chapter of the letter begins with Paul urging Timothy to stay in Ephesus to command the opponents not to teach what is different (μὴ ἑτεροδιδασκαλεῖν, 1:3), implying that there is teaching that is true and correct. Some have suggested that these different teachings are a form of Gnosticism.[40] Although

---

38. ἐξετράπησαν also describes the false teachers in 1:6 who have turned aside to foolish talking.
39. Winter, "Providentia," 84.
40. Brox, *Die Pastoralbriefe*, 32–37; Dibelius and Conzelmann, *Pastoral Epistles*, 17; Oberlinner, *Die Pastoralbriefe*, 3.52–73; Roloff, *Der erste Brief an Timotheus*, 15, 234–36.

Egbert Schlarb has highlighted the parallels between "myths and endless genealogies" (v. 4) found in both the Pentateuch and Philo and argues for a strongly Jewish background, Dillon Thornton and Michel Gourgues caution against jumping to this conclusion.[41] The "law" of 1:8–10 is the Mosaic law.[42] This is supported by the desire of the opponents to be "teachers of the law" (v. 7; cf. Luke 5:17; Acts 5:34) and the structuring of verses 9 and 10 to reflect the Decalogue.[43] The result of the muddled-headed teaching is the wrong focus; their preoccupation with myths and genealogies produces speculations instead of giving their attention to God's plans for the world (ἢ οἰκονομίαν θεοῦ τὴν ἐν πίστει, v. 4).[44]

Not only is the content of their teaching false, the opponents lack the skill to use the law correctly (1:8). In this context, the law is directed at lawbreakers and rebels to punish sin, but the so-called teachers are failing to use the law for its intended purpose.[45]

After digressions in verses 8–11 and 12–17, Paul returns to the issue of false teaching in verses 18–20, and once again demonstrates its effects. In contrast to those who receive eternal life (v. 16) stand the examples of Hymenaeus and Alexander who have shipwrecked their faith (τὴν πίστιν, v. 19) because they rejected a good conscience. Although the grammar points to faith as the objective body of truth, the active rejection of good conscience also suggests a subjective element to what happened.[46] Rather than drive too big a wedge between the objective and subjective elements of faith, the text suggests they are interconnected; that is, their shipwrecking of personal faith is connected to the abandoning of the objective body of truth and practice.[47] First Timothy 1 signals a wrong type of integration as a lack of skill and false teaching produce a wrong focus and ultimately a loss of faith.

---

41. Schlarb, *Die gesunde Lehre*, 86–89; See also Spicq, *Les Épîtres pastorales*, 1.85–119; Thornton, *Hostility in the House of God*, 40–48; Gourgues, *Lettres*, 71.
42. Contra Houlden, *Pastoral Epistles*, 53–58; Saarinen, *Pastoral Epistles*, 38.
43. Lock, *Critical and Exegetical Commentary*, 11–12; Mounce, *Pastoral Epistles*, 31–34; Bernard, *Pastoral Epistles*, 27.
44. Thornton, *Hostility in the House of God*, 39–40, 48.
45. Rosner, *Paul and the Law*, 73–76. The use of the law for the believer is not addressed.
46. Witherington, *Letters and Homilies*, 209.
47. Mutschler, *Glaube in den Pastoralbriefen*, 312; for a survey of scholarly views of "faith" in the LTT, see pp. 5–35.

The impact of false teaching is again on view in chapter 4. Verses 1 and 2 emphasize the apostasy of people from "the faith" to pursue the teachings of demons and lies from false teachers. False teaching also sears the consciences of those who propagate it (v. 2), echoing the rejection of a good conscience by Hymenaeus and Alexander (1:19–20) and reinforcing the importance of maintaining a good conscience (1:5). In a form of asceticism, the false teachers ban marriage and eating certain foods (v. 3).[48] In our earlier discussion of congregational life we have already noted the impact of this teaching on the younger widows, leading some of them to abandon Christ and follow Satan (5:15).

Again, in chapter 6 Paul highlights the impact of false teaching. As in 1:3, there are those who teach what is contrary (ἑτεροδιδασκαλεῖ) to sound doctrine and to teaching that accords with godliness (v. 3). "Sound doctrine" (*hygiainousin logois* ὑγιαίνουσιν λόγοις) emphasizes the healthiness of belief and behaviour being integrated.[49] By contrast, the result of false teaching is a fascination with controversy and disputes, and ungodly behaviour that manifests itself in slander, envy, and the love of money (vv. 4–5, 9–10). The net result is that some people have abandoned the faith and caused themselves great pain (v. 10).

The letter of 1 Timothy demonstrates the devastating effects of the failure to integrate sound theology with godly character. False teaching sears the consciences of those who promote it. It also leads people away from God's priorities to focus on the wrong issues, and produces ungodly behaviour. Ultimately, false teaching results in the abandonment of the faith. The wrong type of integration stems from untrue theology and results in ungodly living and ministry.

---

48. Towner suggests this was a call to a pre-fall Eden, in which there was no sex and no meat, as a preparation for heaven. Towner, *Letters to Timothy and Titus*, 295.

49. Saarinen, *Pastoral Epistles*, 40. For discussion of the metaphor of health and disease, see Malherbe, *Paul and the Popular Philosophers*, 121–36.

Summary

First Timothy clearly points to the integration of theology, skills, and character in the life of Timothy, who is to be a model for the congregation and, by extension, its leaders. Integration is also seen in the overseers and deacons, who are to be above reproach and hold to the truth of the gospel. In addition, they are to also display skills, especially leadership and teaching. Paul's identity, skills, character, and purpose and practice of ministry are integrated with his understanding of God's grace and plan of salvation centred on Christ.

Within the church, all believers are to integrate sound theology and godliness, and so produce people qualified to act as overseers and deacons. This stands in contrast to false teaching which mishandles the Scriptures and so is distracted from God's plan by myths and speculations, thereby producing seared consciences, greed, slander, and envy, and ultimately destroying the faith of people and producing ungodliness.

Therefore, based on our examination of 1 Timothy, we can say that the integration of theology, skills, and character does occur in the letter. In addition, identity and ministry are also integrated. Integration is focused on Timothy, as Paul's delegate, and those who aspire to be overseers and deacons. Integration is needed for those who will lead the congregation.

Integration and the Purpose of 1 Timothy

It is important to understand how the evidence for integration fits within the purpose of 1 Timothy. Paul states his purpose in writing in 3:14–15:[50]

> I hope to come to you soon, but I am writing these instructions to you so that, if I am delayed, you may know how one ought to behave in the household of God, which is the church of the living God, the pillar and bulwark of the truth.

The letter is addressed to Timothy, which is indicated by *soi* (σοι) as the indirect object of *graphō* (γράφω, v. 14) and the second person singular *eidēs* (εἰδῇς, v.

---

50. Fee argues that 1 Tim 1:13 sums up both the purpose and the occasion of the letter. See Fee, *1 & 2 Timothy, Titus*, 10. However, Tomlinson ("Purpose and Stewardship Theme," 59) says 3:14–16 is an explicit statement of purpose for writing. See also Krause, *1 Timothy*, 74; Köstenberger, *1–2 Timothy & Titus*, 56–57; Bassler, *1 Timothy, 2 Timothy, Titus*, 72.

15).⁵¹ This is reinforced by the greeting addressed to Timothy in 1:2, the closing exhortation to him in 6:20, and the second person singular verbs directed to Timothy, especially in the second half of the letter (e.g. 4:6, 7, 11, 12; 5:1, 3, 7; 6:2, 11, 12).⁵² Alongside this are Paul's closing words "Grace be with you" (6:21), with the plural *hymōn* (ὑμῶν) indicating that he expects the letter to be read to the whole congregation. The letter therefore is a detailed and focused address to Timothy which, through him, speaks also to the congregation.⁵³ This combination of focus on Timothy and on the church is also on display in Paul's statement of purpose in 3:14–15. Timothy needs to know these things (Ταῦτά, v. 14) for his own sake and for the sake of the congregation. Therefore, Timothy is to teach these things (Ταῦτα, 4:6) to the church so they will live in keeping with their identity as the household of God who hold to and promote the truth, resulting in *eusebeia*. This happens in the context of false teaching.

The evidence for integration fits within the purpose of 1 Timothy. Timothy is to pay attention to the integration of sound teaching and godliness in his own life (4:6–8, 16). Timothy is then to model and teach the integration of sound theology, skills, and godly character to the whole congregation (4:12, 15) with the expectation that the church will integrate the truth of God's word with godly living. It is also expected that people appointed to the roles of overseer and deacon will show integration of theology, skills, and character. Timothy teaches and models integration, as do the overseers and deacons, so that the church will integrate theology and godliness. Integrated leadership is necessary so that believers may know how to behave in the household of God. Integration fits squarely with the purpose of 1 Timothy.

---

51. Perkins, *Pastoral Letters*, 68–69.
52. See the table in Yarbrough, *Timothy and Titus*, 235.
53. The intended recipients of each of the LTT are much debated. For example, Witherington, *Letters and Homilies*, 1, 67, says they are private letters "not composed for oral delivery to a congregation." By contrast, Dibelius and Conzelmann, *Pastoral Epistles*, 1, say the contents of the LTT "are not intended for the addressee, but for the people." Gourgues says 1 Timothy and Titus are focused on communities and 2 Timothy is a personal letter. See Gourgues, *Lettres*, 29–37. For each of the LTT, I will take the position that it is addressed primarily to individuals but intended to be read to the congregation. See Collins, *Timothy and Titus*, 7; Kelly, *Pastoral Epistles*, 2; Fee, *1 & 2 Timothy, Titus*, 10; Towner, *Letters to Timothy and Titus*, 35.

Discussion Questions

1. What is the content of integration in your context?

2. First Timothy highlights the importance of
    - godliness;
    - high levels of skill in the managing and leading of people, as well as teaching;
    - sound doctrine.

   Which of these is most surprising to you?

3. First Timothy points to the inclusion of identity and ministry (as well as theology, skills, and character) as part of integration. How might identity and ministry be incorporated in your context?

4. "Timothy teaches and models integration, as do the overseers and deacons, so that the church will integrate theology and godliness. Integrated leadership is necessary so that believers may know how to behave in the household of God." What are the implications of this for theological education?

4

What Is Integrated in 2 Timothy and Titus?

As in the previous chapter, we are again looking for evidence of *what* is integrated in the letters of 2 Timothy and Titus. At the end of the chapter, we draw some observations based on what we have examined across the LTT.

2 Timothy
Focus Passage: 2 Timothy 2:14–26

> [14] Remind them of this, and warn them before God that they are to avoid wrangling over words, which does no good but only ruins those who are listening. [15] Do your best to present yourself to God as one approved by him, a worker who has no need to be ashamed, rightly explaining the word of truth. [16] Avoid profane chatter, for it will lead people into more and more impiety, [17] and their talk will spread like gangrene. Among them are Hymenaeus and Philetus, [18] who have swerved from the truth by claiming that the resurrection has already taken place. They are upsetting the faith of some. [19] But God's firm foundation stands, bearing this inscription: "The Lord knows those who are his," and, "Let everyone who calls on the name of the Lord turn away from wickedness."
>
> [20] In a large house there are utensils not only of gold and silver but also of wood and clay, some for special use, some for ordinary. [21] All who cleanse themselves of the things I have mentioned will become special utensils, dedicated and useful to the owner of the

house, ready for every good work. ²² Shun youthful passions and pursue righteousness, faith, love, and peace, along with those who call on the Lord from a pure heart. ²³ Have nothing to do with stupid and senseless controversies; you know that they breed quarrels. ²⁴ And the Lord's servant must not be quarrelsome but kindly to everyone, an apt teacher, patient, ²⁵ correcting opponents with gentleness. God may perhaps grant that they will repent and come to know the truth, ²⁶ and that they may escape from the snare of the devil, having been held captive by him to do his will.

In 2 Timothy 2:14, Timothy is to remind the congregation of "this," that is, the sound theology of Paul's gospel (v. 8), which is the word of God (v. 9) and is summarized in the faithful saying of 2:11–13. This will require Timothy to handle God's word of truth (τὸν λόγον τῆς ἀληθείας, v. 15) with skill and precision, literally, "cutting it straight" (ὀρθοτομοῦντα), like a highly competent worker (ἐργάτην).[1] He must also avoid ungodliness (ἀσεβείας, v. 16), knowing that God's people are sealed as his own and therefore must live godly lives and turn aside from sin (v. 19), by pursuing righteousness, love, faith, and peace (v. 22). By cleansing himself, he will be useful in God's service, and "ready for every good work" (v. 21).[2] Timothy is to display godly character as he deals with opponents by being kind, patient, and gentle instead of quarrelsome. He must demonstrate skill by being an apt teacher (διδακτικόν, v. 24), and the content of his teaching is to be the knowledge of the truth (ἐπίγνωσιν ἀληθείας, v. 25), both of which reinforce the earlier exhortation of verse 15 for the skilful teaching of God's word. Smith sums up what Paul is looking for in Timothy by saying that "qualification for teaching involved not only orthodoxy of content but godliness of character and competency and skill in communicating truth."[3] Timothy is to integrate theology, skills, and character.

---

1. BDAG, s.v. "ὀρθοτομέω"; C. Spicq, "ὀρθοτομέω," *TLNT*, 2.595. The background of the metaphor is debated, though the overall thrust is clear. See Marshall, *Pastoral Epistles*, 748–49, for options.
2. Note the repetition of the phrase "every good work" (πᾶν ἔργον ἀγαθόν) in 2 Tim 2:21 and 3:17. Preparation for "every good work" involves cleansing oneself of sin and being equipped by the Scriptures.
3. Smith, *Pauline Communities*, 74.

Other Passages Directed to Timothy

An example of the integration of identity with theology, skills, and character is also found in 2 Timothy 3:14–17. "The man of God" (ESV; ᾗ ὁ τοῦ θεοῦ ἄνθρωπος, v. 17) primarily refers to Timothy and links him (and by implication those who will follow Timothy, such as the "faithful people" of 2 Tim 2:2) to a heritage of Old Testament prophetic figures and so highlights the authoritative role his teaching has in the life of God's people.[4] Timothy is to remain faithful to the truth of the Scriptures which bring salvation and educate in godliness (vv. 14–16). The *hina* (ἵνα) of verse 17 indicates the goal of using the God-breathed Scriptures, namely, that Timothy is to be "proficient" (NRSV) or "complete" (ESV) (ἄρτιος), and "equipped for every good work" (πρὸς πᾶν ἔργον ἀγαθὸν ἐξηρτισμένος). The adjective *artios* (ἄρτιος) carries nuances of being proficient and capable, completely suited for the task presented.[5] The context suggests that "every good work" includes righteous living and the tasks of Christian ministry such as teaching (v. 16), while the same phrase occurs in 2 Timothy 2:21 and encompasses all Christian living.[6] Timothy's identity as "the man of God" is integrated with his faithfulness to right theology, proficiency for the task, and every good work of life and ministry. He is equipped for this by the Scriptures and is to equip others in the same way.

Further evidence for integration in the life of Timothy is found in 2:1–7. He is to maintain correct theology, with "these things" (ταῦτα, v. 2) functioning as an all-encompassing term for the content taught by Paul (v. 2). Just as the Lord had entrusted (τὴν παραθήκην μου, 1:12) Paul with the good deposit (τὴν καλὴν παραθήκην, 1:14) of the gospel, so now Timothy was to entrust (παράθου) "faithful people" (πιστοῖς ἀνθρώποις) with the apostolic truth. This implies a high level of skill which Timothy was to employ for the successful transmission of the gospel to the next generation of leaders. It was more than passing on information; "entrusting" involved equipping the "faithful people" in such a way that they in turn would be able to teach others. In addition, Timothy is urged to suffer as a good soldier of Christ (v. 3) empowered by the grace found in Christ (v. 1). Three metaphors describe what this looks like in

---

4. Towner, *Letters to Timothy and Titus*, 592–93; Bassler, *1 Timothy, 2 Timothy, Titus*, 168–69.
5. Perkins, *Pastoral Letters*, 220; Marshall, *Pastoral Epistles*, 796.
6. Towner, *Letters to Timothy and Titus*, 594.

practice: the soldier of verse 4 suggests undistracted obedience, the athlete highlights ethical conduct, and the farmer points to the hard work required.[7] Timothy integrates this godly character with right theology and the skill to entrust the gospel to others.

Second Timothy 4:1–5 also possibly suggests Timothy is to integrate theology, skills, and character. Timothy is to teach right theology. In the first of five imperatives in verse 2, Paul commands Timothy to "preach the word" (NIV; κήρυξον τὸν λόγον). In the context, the most immediate content this could refer to is the Scriptures and the teaching received from Paul (3:14–17).[8] "The word" is in keeping with "the word of God" (2:9) that brings salvation because it is "the word of truth" (2:15).[9] Just as Paul was appointed a herald (κῆρυξ, 1:11), Timothy is now charged with preaching (κήρυξον, v. 2) the same content; he must "convince, rebuke, and encourage, with the utmost patience in teaching" (v. 2). Verses 3 and 4 contain repeated concepts: Timothy is to continue this ministry despite the anticipated rejection of sound doctrine and the truth in favour of myths, and the many teachers who teach what people want to hear (vv. 3–4).[10] Sound doctrine is that which promotes spiritual health.[11] Thus "the word," "the sound doctrine," and "the truth" stand in parallel in consecutive verses. Timothy is to consistently maintain right theology even in the face of opposition.

This passage also points to qualities of Timothy's character. He is to "always be sober" (νῆφε ἐν πᾶσιν, v. 5), with the *en pasin* underscoring that sobriety is a metaphor carrying the sense of "being alert and controlled with regard to one's speech and conduct."[12] He is also to endure suffering (v. 5).

---

7. Bray, *Pastoral Epistles*, 351–55.
8. Smith, *Pauline Communities*, 171.
9. Swinson, *What Is Scripture?*, 138.
10. Smith and Dickson agree that the NT usage of κηρύσσω relates to gospel proclamation and that this is possible both inside and outside the congregation. However, Dickson's argument that the focus of Timothy's preaching of the word is beyond the congregation does not take adequate account of the opposition from false teachers within the congregation (2:14–26; 3:1–9) who need to hear the gospel. Timothy was to preach the gospel both inside and beyond the congregation. See Smith, *Pauline Communities*, 166, 171–72; Dickson, *Mission-Commitment*, 322–26.
11. Hutson, *Timothy and Titus*, 199.
12. Gloer, *1 & 2 Timothy-Titus*, 299; Collins, *Timothy and Titus*, 271; Johnson, *Letters to Timothy*, 430.

Timothy is also to be involved in the work of evangelism (ἔργον ποίησον εὐαγγελιστοῦ, v. 5), which Samuel Ngewa regards as a skill Timothy has learned.[13] William Mounce says evangelism is the gift Timothy received from God (1:6).[14] This is possible given that Ephesians 4:11 says evangelists are a gift to God's church. However, the context emphasizes not the skill or gift but the task, preaching the gospel.[15] The *gar* (γὰρ) of verse 6 links what follows to provide the reason why Timothy must evangelize; Paul recognizes that his departure is near and Timothy must take over the responsibility of gospel proclamation.

Cumulatively, 2 Timothy 4:1–5 demonstrates that Timothy must hold to and preach the word of truth, continue in good conduct, and engage in evangelism. This points to the integration of theology and character in his life, but whether evangelism should be regarded as a skill or gift is less certain, even though it was clearly something Timothy was to do.

There are also other indications of integration focused on Timothy throughout the letter. In 2 Timothy 1:8–9, God's saving and gracious calling through Christ applies to Timothy as well as Paul (ἡμᾶς / ἡμῖν, v. 9), and it is on this basis that Paul urges Timothy to be willing to suffer for the gospel just as Paul is already doing.[16] This willingness to suffer will translate into not being ashamed of the message about the Lord or the Lord's messenger Paul (v. 8). As with Paul, Timothy is to integrate theology with suffering.

Another indication of integration is found in 2 Timothy 1:13–14. Timothy is to guard "the good deposit" (NIV; τὴν καλὴν παραθήκην, v. 14) in the strength of the Holy Spirit.[17] The good deposit is the pattern of sound doctrine (ὑγιαινόντων λόγων, v. 13) that Paul has passed on to Timothy. Timothy's conviction about the theological health of the gospel will lead him to protect its contents. As Timothy guards the gospel, he will conduct himself in a godly manner, "in the faith and love that are in Christ Jesus" (v. 13). Thus, theological convictions, behaviour in guarding the gospel, and the manner of conduct are integrated.

---

13. Ngewa, *1 & 2 Timothy and Titus*, 297.
14. Mounce, *Pastoral Epistles*, 576.
15. Bassler, *1 Timothy, 2 Timothy, Titus*, 170; Collins, *Timothy and Titus*, 272; Simpson, *Pastoral Epistles*, 227; Weiser, *Der zweite Brief an Timotheusw*, 304.
16. Wolter, "Der Apostel und sein Schüler," 27–28.
17. Weiser, *Der zweite Brief an Timotheus*, 16, 127–28; Lau, *Manifest in Flesh*, 28.

As Timothy serves the church, 2 Timothy 2:24–26; 3:14–17; and 2:1–7 provide clear evidence that he is to demonstrate the integration of right theology, skilful handling of the word of truth, and godly character reflecting his identity as "the man of God." This is reinforced by 4:1–5 in which sound doctrine, right character, and evangelism are joined together. He will not only live a godly life; he will conduct ministry in a godly and ethical manner (2:24) in contrast to his opponents (3:6). In addition, his willingness to guard the gospel and suffer for it, and yet still be undistracted, ethical, and hardworking, is an additional indication of the integration of theology and behaviour.

"Faithful People"

Paul calls on Timothy to identify a group of "faithful people" (πιστοῖς ἀνθρώποις) to entrust with the gospel (2 Tim 2:2). Their description as "faithful" within the context of the letter suggests they are faithful to the content of the gospel (e.g. as in the "faithful word," 2:11) as well as faithful to the ethical standards of the gospel, and the manner in which they conducted ministry was also important (2:14).[18] People of good character were essential.[19] Just as the Lord had entrusted (τὴν παραθήκην μου, 1:12) Paul with the good deposit (τὴν καλὴν παραθήκην, 1:14) of the gospel, so now Timothy was to entrust (παράθου) "faithful people" with the apostolic truth. In addition, they will be competent to teach others (ἱκανοὶ ἔσονται καὶ ἑτέρους διδάξαι). The adjective *hikanoi* (ἱκανοὶ) carries the sense of giftedness and aptitude, which Ceslas Spicq says is coupled with God's empowering.[20]

Paul and Timothy are facing the challenge of developing a new generation of leaders in the congregation. Timothy is to entrust the gospel to people of good character who will not distort its message and will be skilful in teaching that message to others as they conduct ministry ethically. The new generation of congregational leaders are to demonstrate the integration of theology, skills, and character.

---

18. 2 Tim 2:14 refers to the "faithful people" of 2 Tim 2:2. Hutson, *Timothy and Titus*, 182; Knight, *Pastoral Epistles*, 411; Köstenberger, *1–2 Timothy & Titus*, 241.
19. Towner, *Letters to Timothy and Titus*, 491; Mounce, *Pastoral Epistles*, 506; Weiser, *Der zweite Brief an Timotheus*, 16, 159.
20. Spicq, "ἱκανός," *TLNT*, 2.221.

Paul

In 2 Timothy 1:8–12, Paul outlines that suffering is integrated with theology, skills, character, and identity. Paul is suffering for the gospel (v. 8), the theological content of which is outlined in verses 9 and 10 and is centred on God's saving grace in Christ Jesus. As a recipient of that grace, and strengthened by God's power (v. 8), Paul is willing to suffer for the sake of the gospel. God has saved Paul by his grace, calling Paul to belong to him (v. 9), and appointing him as a herald, apostle, and teacher of the gospel (v. 11). Paul identifies himself, not as a prisoner of the Roman Empire, but as the Lord's prisoner (τὸν δέσμιον αὐτοῦ, v. 8), and therefore he is not ashamed of the testimony of the Lord (v. 8). Paul is secure in the understanding that his life and the gospel are safe because the Lord is powerful and able (δυνατός, v. 12).[21] The title "teacher" (v. 11) also implies Paul has a high degree of skill.[22] Thus, gospel theology, suffering, personal identity, skills, and ministry are integrated together as Paul languishes in gaol.

The integration of theology and suffering in Paul's life is also evident in 2 Timothy 2:8–13. Paul is suffering for the gospel (v. 9), with verse 8 providing a summary of its contents. He is willing to suffer so that God's people may receive the salvation available in Christ Jesus (v. 10). Paul provides the theological basis for his endurance in the solemn trustworthy saying of verses 11–13.

A broader perspective of integration in Paul's life is seen in 2 Timothy 3:10–14. The list in verses 10 and 11 is governed by the "my" (μου) of verse 10. In keeping with Paul's use of *mou* in 1:12 and 2:8, "my teaching" (μου τῇ διδασκαλίᾳ) would indicate Paul's personal commitment to the content of truth deposited in the gospel of Jesus. Paul's character has also been observable – his conduct, love, personal faith, and purpose in life. Alongside this is his endurance in the face of suffering and persecution. Verse 14 also points to Paul's skill in teaching and training, as Timothy is to continue in what he has learned (ἔμαθες) and believes, knowing from whom he has learned (ἔμαθες) it. The people Timothy has learned from include his mother and

---

21. Whether v. 12 refers to what Paul has entrusted to God or what God has entrusted to Paul is debated. The μου suggests the former possibility, the repetition of τὴν παραθήκην in v. 14 the latter. What is not disputed is that Paul's confidence rests on the Lord's power, not his own. For a survey see Knight, *Pastoral Epistles*, 379–80.
22. White, *Where Is the Wise Man?*, 143–48; Maurice, *Teacher in Ancient Rome*, 140.

grandmother (v. 15; 1:5) and Paul (vv. 10–11). The verb "to learn" (μανθάνω) means "to gain knowledge or skill by instruction."[23] Paul has skilfully taught Timothy in a way that enables him to persevere in the face of opposition, false teaching, and ungodly living (3:1–5, 12), and has equipped him to pass the gospel on to new leaders (2:2). The combination of theology, personal character, skills, and perseverance is both in keeping with the integration identified in earlier passages and adds further texture to the portrait of Paul by highlighting his purposeful and loving way of life.

Perseverance to the end is also a theme of chapter 4. In verse 7, Paul says he has "kept the faith." At this point, "the faith" (τὴν πίστιν) carries both subjective and objective dimensions. Paul has kept trusting in the truth he has preserved.[24] As he looks forward, his incentive for persevering is the crown of righteousness he will be awarded at the appearing of the Lord (v. 8). As Paul reviews his past, he understands that the Lord has strengthened him so that he might complete the task of proclaiming the gospel (v. 17). In context, the emphasis of *to kērygma* (τὸ κήρυγμα) falls on the activity of proclamation, though the content cannot be excluded. The point of the proclamation is that all the nations might hear.[25] The phrase "all the nations" (πάντα τὰ ἔθνη) is used of God's covenant with Abraham to bless the nations through him (Gen 18:18).[26] This places Paul's apostolic task squarely within God's plan of salvation. Having completed the task, Paul is confident God will bring him into his heavenly kingdom (v. 18).

Second Timothy demonstrates a strong and consistent emphasis on the integration of theology and suffering in the life of Paul. Paul is willing to suffer for the truth of the gospel and to persevere both in personal trust in the Lord and in the ministry of proclamation entrusted to him. He does this for the salvation of God's people and the nations. The picture of integration is further filled out to include Paul's loving conduct and purposeful life, and his sense

---

23. BDAG, s.v. "μανθάνω."
24. Knight, *Pastoral Epistles*, 460.
25. καὶ is epexegetical. Mounce, *Pastoral Epistles*, 596; Knight, *Pastoral Epistles*, 470.
26. Köstenberger, "Investigation of the Mission Motif," 58–59. This picks up the original promise of Gen 12:3 in which "all peoples [πᾶσαι αἱ φυλαὶ] on earth will be blessed through you" (NIV). Although the wording is different, the concept is the same.

of personal identity. Theology, skill, godly character, ministry, and personal identity are integrated in the apostle Paul.

The Church

The church provides the pool of people from whom the "faithful people" are drawn, suggesting that integration should be evident in the congregation, and the plural address in 2 Timothy 4:22 points to them being aware of Paul's expectations and instructions. While the church is not mentioned very often in 2 Timothy, there is evidence of the integration of theology, godly character, and perseverance.

The trustworthy saying of 2:11–13 contains a succession of first person plural verbs, referring to "the elect" of verse 10, making it applicable to Paul, the whole church, and all believers, and providing them with their identity. The structure moves from the past to the present to the future.[27] Dying now and living with Christ in the future (v. 11b) parallels the salvation with eternal glory in Christ Jesus (v. 10).[28] Believers who endure (present tense) will participate in Christ's eschatological reign (future tense). By contrast, eschatological judgment awaits those who apostatize in the present. The implication is that the identity and faithful endurance of all believers are theologically grounded in the faithfulness of Christ and the salvation he offers.

This is reinforced in 2 Timothy 2:19 which quotes from the LXX of Numbers 16:5. In the face of false teaching about the resurrection (v. 18), believers can be secure in the Lord's faithfulness to his people because he knows them. The corollary of being known by God is that believers who call Jesus their Lord must shun wickedness (v. 19).[29] Theology, identity, and godly behaviour are to be integrated for all believers.

Godly behaviour will result in persecution (3:12) and this applies to all (πάντες) believers, not just Paul and Timothy as discussed earlier. The nuance worth noting at this point is that rather than gospel proclamation (1:8–12) or holding to the truth (4:2–5) producing suffering, in this case it is godly living

---

27. Witherington, *Letters and Homilies*, 332.
28. This reflects the sense of dying to self and being united with Christ in Rom 6:8. Marshall, *Pastoral Epistles*, 739; Towner, *Letters to Timothy and Titus*, 509.
29. Bray, *Pastoral Epistles*, 379.

(ζῆν εὐσεβῶς) that will result in persecution. Given that godly living is expected of all Christians, Paul is saying that persecution should also be expected.

Another theological incentive to persevere in the faith is the prospect of the crown of righteousness to be presented by the Lord as righteous judge (4:8). Paul makes a point of saying this reward is for all (πᾶσιν) believers who have longed for the appearing of Christ at his return.

Paul also singles out Onesiphorus as a member of the congregation (4:19) worthy of commendation. Onesiphorus was not ashamed of Paul being in gaol and therefore searched hard to find him (1:16–17). In the light of Paul's exhortation that Timothy should not be ashamed of the gospel or of Paul as the Lord's gospel messenger, Onesiphorus's lack of shame regarding Paul should be understood as evidence of the integration of convictions about the gospel and personal action. Onesiphorus believes the gospel and, in the light of it, looked for Paul even in prison.

The integration of theology and perseverance in the face of persecution is a consistent theme that is applied to the whole church in 2 Timothy. Endurance comes from a right theological understanding of relationship with Christ, and the eschatological reward he will give is the incentive to persevere. The integration of belief and behaviour is exemplified in Onesiphorus. Thus, what is expected to be integrated in the church is in keeping with what is expected of its leaders; the church provides an appropriate pool from which to develop new integrated leadership.

Signs of the Wrong Type of Integration

The letter also paints a picture of what the wrong type of integration looks like. In contrast to Paul's exhortation that Timothy join him in suffering is the lack of willingness to identify with Paul and his gospel. No one supported Paul at his first trial, but instead all abandoned him (4:16), and now, as he writes to Timothy, everyone in the province of Asia has deserted him, including Phygelus, Hermogenes (1:15), and Demas (4:10). The theological reason for Demas's desertion is his love for the current age, indicating that he has failed to integrate knowledge of the gospel with a godly life that is willing to suffer by identifying with God's gospel messenger Paul (3:12). This stands in contrast to Onesiphorus's willingness to identify with Paul in gaol (1:16–18).

Another sign of the wrong type of integration is false teaching and its effects. The content of the false teaching is the claim that the final resurrection has already happened (2:18), which both opposes the truth (3:8) and is a departure from it (2:17). This is an abandonment of sound doctrine that produces spiritual health (4:3). Turning aside from the truth in favour of listening to the myths is characteristic of this age and is sadly something Timothy is to expect (4:3–4).[30] Opposing the truth corrupts the minds of the false teachers (3:8) and, as their false teaching spreads, drawing in more people, it results in increasing ungodliness (2:16–17) and a rise in quarrelling in the congregation (2:14, 23). The false teachers focus their ministry on women who are vulnerable (3:6).[31] Ultimately, false teaching destroys the faith of some members of the church (2:14, 18).

As well as distorting the content of the message, the false teachers lack skill in teaching. Given that some of the women in the church are "always being instructed and can never arrive at a knowledge of the truth" (3:7), it suggests that those teaching them are not only theologically corrupt but also incompetent, and stands in contrast to Timothy, Paul, and the "faithful people" who all display the ability to teach others.

The false teachers also integrate the wrong type of character and this is described in 3:1–5. Their love will be distorted, loving themselves and money and pleasure, but hating what is good and failing to love God. This will manifest itself in the way they relate to God (blasphemy, lacking holiness) and to other people (arrogant boasting, disobedient to parents, slandering, and betraying others). The indictment of their character is summarized as "holding to the outward form of godliness but denying its power" (3:5).[32]

Summary

The letter of 2 Timothy provides evidence of integration as Timothy is to hold to sound doctrine, handle the word of truth with skill, do the work of an evangelist, and be godly in character in keeping with his identity as "the

---

30. Elengabeka, "La Rhétorique de la temporalité," 392–93.
31. Zamfir says the women "are both victims of the false teachers (since they are captivated by them) and sinners themselves." Zamfir, *Men and Women*, 190.
32. Thornton, *Hostility in the House of God*, 203, argues that the opponents have renounced the Holy Spirit and so are powerless.

man of God." Similarly, the "faithful people" he is to train up are to be of good character, committed to the truth, and competent to teach it. Second Timothy supports the hypothesis that integration involves theology, skills, and character, and in addition connects this with the willingness to suffer for the gospel.

Bearing the identity of God's people, all Christians will be persecuted simply for living a godly life (ζῆν εὐσεβῶς, 3:12). In addition, there seems to be another "layer" of hardship that comes with being a teacher and proclaimer of God's word. Paul is already suffering for the gospel and urges Timothy to join him (1:8). Timothy is to endure hardship, as are the "faithful people" (2:2–3; 4:5), with the willingness to persevere in the face of opposition and persecution being theologically motivated. The gospel of grace in Christ Jesus is God's word that brings salvation, so it is worth guarding and proclaiming (1:13; 2:10, 25; 4:2–5, 16) in the knowledge that people are accountable to Jesus the eschatological judge, who will reward those who persevere in faith. The importance of the integration of sound theology and perseverance in the face of suffering is magnified in 2 Timothy by its contrast with false teaching which distorts the truth and leads to godless behaviour and an unwillingness to persevere in the faith, suffer for the gospel, or identify with those who do.

Integration and the Purpose of 2 Timothy

In recent years, a number of scholars have challenged the consensus that 2 Timothy is the most personal of the LTT, written as Paul faces imminent death and therefore like a last will and testament.[33] Ben Witherington and Luke Timothy Johnson argue the letter is not testamentary because, rather than Paul passing on the baton to Timothy, they are of the same generation, and there is no mention of Paul's death.[34] Michael Prior says that "being poured out" (σπένδομαι, 4:6) is not a reference to Paul's death but to him giving himself in service of the gospel.[35] In addition, Craig Smith has argued that neither 2 Timothy 4:1–8 nor the letter as a whole conforms to the literary conventions

---

33. Examples of the consensus include Marshall, *Pastoral Epistles*, 39; Bassler, *1 Timothy, 2 Timothy, Titus*, 22; Fiore, *Pastoral Epistles*, 9; Mounce, *Pastoral Epistles*, 577; Quinn and Wacker, *Letters to Timothy*, 775–76; Knight, *Pastoral Epistles*, 458–59; Köstenberger, *1–2 Timothy & Titus*, 203–4.
34. Witherington, *Letters and Homilies*, 303–4; Johnson, *Letters to Timothy*, 321–22.
35. Prior, *Paul the Letter-Writer*, 92–98.

of a farewell speech or testament but displays features of a charge and should be treated as such.[36] Paul is not anticipating his death but his release from prison.[37] Hulitt Gloer opts for a middle of the road position recognizing both testamentary and personal elements, and so categorizes 2 Timothy as a "personal paraenetic letter."[38]

However, across the debates surrounding the nature of Paul's circumstances and the genre of the letter, consistent themes emerge about the purpose of 2 Timothy. For example, David Beck, building on the work of Witherington and Prior, states that

> the purpose of 2 Timothy is best understood as a letter of encouragement and exhortation to Timothy, knowing the difficulty of the opposition he faced, from Paul who himself knew firsthand about difficult circumstances and suffering. It is an exhortation to faithfulness to the gospel, the word God has revealed.[39]

Dibelius and Conzelmann say that in writing 2 Timothy "Paul sets himself up as an example of suffering in order to encourage Timothy to similar endurance."[40] Alan Tomlinson argues that Paul's purpose in writing is to call Timothy to Rome, and to charge him to follow his example of godliness, guard the gospel, and pass it on to others.[41] Fiore says, "Like Acts 20:17–38, 2 Timothy uses Paul's last will and testament to address the community situation of conflict between orthodoxy and heresy. The letter aims to embolden the audience to cling fast to the Pauline tradition in thought and action against those Paul 'predicted' would deviate from it."[42] The scholarly consensus is that Paul is writing to exhort and encourage Timothy (and through him, the congregation, including the "faithful people") because faithfulness to the gospel will require endurance in the face of opposition from false teachers. Timothy is not to be ashamed of the gospel

---

36. Smith, *Timothy's Task, Paul's Prospect*, 146–47. Also note Smith's critique of Prior for not adequately appreciating metaphorical language on pp. 111–14.
37. Smith, *Timothy's Task, Paul's Prospect*, 127–45.
38. Gloer, *1 & 2 Timothy-Titus*, 11.
39. Beck, "Linguistic Features," 97.
40. Dibelius and Conzelmann, *Pastoral Epistles*, 7.
41. Tomlinson, "Purpose and Stewardship Theme," 63.
42. Fiore, *Pastoral Epistles*, 9.

but to continue in what he has known and believed (1:13; 3:14), guarding the gospel (1:14), suffering for it (1:8), and passing it on (2:2).

In view of Paul's looming departure (whether death or release from prison), Timothy must take up the baton and pursue a similar path to that of the apostle. He also must preach the word regardless of circumstances, keeping the pattern of sound teaching. He is to do it with skill, rightly handling the word of God, with an ongoing commitment to evangelism. And he is to avoid godless behaviour, instead being pure in the pursuit of righteousness, faith, love, and peace (2:22). Guarding the gospel, suffering for it, and passing it on, will require Timothy to integrate theology, skills, and character with perseverance and suffering. It is Timothy's task to train and equip others so they can be entrusted with the gospel (2:2), and the evidence points to the expectation that they also must integrate theology, skills, and godly character. We have also seen that Paul's expectation of the church is that they will integrate sound theology and godly character and persevere in the face of persecution.

The chain of passing on the gospel from Paul to Timothy to faithful leaders and the church makes clear this implication: only leaders who have integrated right theology, skills, and godly behaviour will do what is needed to guard, suffer for, and pass on the gospel to the next generation. Integration is important to the purposes of 2 Timothy.

Titus
Focus Passage: Titus 1:5–9

> [5] I left you behind in Crete for this reason, that you should put in order what remained to be done, and should appoint elders in every town, as I directed you: [6] someone who is blameless, married only once, whose children are believers, not accused of debauchery and not rebellious. [7] For a bishop, as God's steward, must be blameless; he must not be arrogant or quick-tempered or addicted to wine or violent or greedy for gain; [8] but he must be hospitable, a lover of goodness, prudent, upright, devout, and self-controlled. [9] He must have a firm grasp of the word that is trustworthy in accordance with the teaching, so that he may be

able both to preach with sound doctrine and to refute those who contradict it.

The qualifications for overseers in Titus 1:5–9 point to the integration of theology, skills, and character.[43] The overseer is "God's steward" (θεοῦ οἰκονόμον, v. 7) and therefore must have blameless character (ἀνέγκλητος, vv. 6–7) which is demonstrated in his relationships with his wife and children (v. 6) and others (v. 7).[44] He is to be motivated by loving what is good rather than seeking dishonest gain (vv. 7–8). Integrated with blameless character is the sound doctrine of the trustworthy message (πιστοῦ λόγου, v. 9) which is God's salvation plan revealed through his word (τὸν λόγον αὐτοῦ, 1:3). "Sound doctrine" (τῇ διδασκαλίᾳ τῇ ὑγιαινούσῃ, v. 9) produces spiritual health and has an integrative effect by bringing together right belief and right behaviour. Starling says "the overseer must not only be a person who knows what is true and does what is good, but one who is a 'lover' of goodness (1:8), with a deep, affectionate commitment to the truth of the gospel and the vision of the good that it teaches."[45]

In addition, Schreiner and John Goodrich identify within the stewardship metaphor the skills of leadership and teaching.[46] Stewardship implies responsibility for others, and stewards of God's people are to exercise their skills in handling God's word (v. 9) with the capacity to encourage, teach, and rebuke, these being the same skills Titus is to use in the life of the congregation (2:15). Tomlinson goes further and argues that Paul has drawn on language and imagery associated with estate stewardship in the Roman world in describing the duties expected of those who lead God's church.[47] Central to the metaphor of stewardship is the concept of trust; the stewards have been entrusted with responsibility for the care of something owned by someone else. Given this

---

43. The terms "elder" (πρεσβυτέρους, v. 5) and "overseer" or "bishop" (ἐπίσκοπον, v. 7) are used to refer to the same role. Köstenberger, *1–2 Timothy & Titus*, 313; Merkle, "Offices, Titles, and Roles." Gourgues, *Lettres*, 364, argues they are distinct but related roles. However, the directive of v. 5. points to there being only one group; i.e. Paul did not call for the appointment of elders and overseers.
44. Note the δεῖ γάρ joining the behaviour with the role, so linking vv. 6 and 7.
45. Starling, "The Scribe," 23.
46. Schreiner, "Overseeing and Serving," 109; Goodrich, "Overseers as Stewards."
47. Tomlinson, "Purpose and Stewardship Theme," 67–83.

trust, they are accountable to the owner and so will need to work hard and skilfully for their master's benefit and praise. While Tomlinson's designation of estate stewardship as the "controlling metaphor" across all the LTT may be claiming too much, nonetheless at this point it evokes the importance of competence and skill for the overseer.[48]

Paul's designation of overseers as God's stewards is therefore a significant metaphor that weaves together theological orthodoxy, responsible and skilful service, and blameless character. God's steward is a picture of someone who has integrated theology, skills, and character for Christian ministry.

Titus

The integration of sound doctrine, skilful teaching and leadership, and godly behaviour is to be embodied by Titus. In contrast to the false teachers (1:16), Titus is directed to "teach what is consistent with sound doctrine" (λάλει ἃ πρέπει τῇ ὑγιαινούσῃ διδασκαλίᾳ, 2:1), with its content being spelled out in 2:11–14 as God's plan of grace in Christ that saves people and transforms the way they live. "Sound doctrine" produces spiritual health, in contrast to the diseased minds and consciences of the false teachers (1:15).[49] This is what Titus is to teach (2:15). Alongside teaching sound doctrine, Titus is to model a godly life of good deeds for the congregation (2:7).

Titus is to be skilful in his teaching (λάλει, 2:1).[50] He must not only pass on doctrinal content but speak in such a way that it produces godly behaviour among the older men (v. 2), older women (v. 3), younger men (v. 6), and slaves (v. 9). His teaching is also to enable the older women to teach the younger women what is good (καλοδιδασκάλους, v. 3).[51] The teaching of Titus is doctrinally sound and produces godly behaviour, and it trains people so they can replicate the same content and lifestyle with others. The combination of

---

48. Tomlinson, 67.
49. Malherbe, "Paraenesis," 301; Bray, *Pastoral Epistles*, 500.
50. The verb λαλέω covers everyday speech and conversation but is flexible in its use. See Smith, *Pauline Communities*, 109.
51. Towner, *Letters to Timothy and Titus*, 724, argues that καλοδιδασκάλους should be translated as "good teachers." This would strengthen our position that teaching involved doing it skilfully. However, both the immediate context and early Christian writings point to the ethical content of the teaching as the favoured translation. See Marshall, *Pastoral Epistles*, 246.

the content and manner of teaching is also on view in 2:7–8, reinforcing that "teaching" involves more than passing on information.[52] The imperatives Paul gives Titus throughout the letter, such as to rebuke (1:13; 2:15), teach (2:1, 15), and encourage (2:6, 15), imply that the skills of leadership and teaching are needed for his ministry, and are in line with what is required of elders.[53]

Paul

The letter of Titus provides evidence that theology, godly character, identity, and ministry are integrated in the life of the apostle Paul. The letter opens with Paul declaring his identity as a "slave of God and an apostle of Jesus Christ" (δοῦλος θεοῦ, ἀπόστολος δὲ Ἰησοῦ Χριστοῦ, 1:1).[54] Often translated as "servant", the term "slave of God" is used of key Old Testament figures such as Abraham (Ps 105:6, 42), Moses (Ps 105:26; cf. Rev 15:3), David (2 Sam 7:5, 8; Pss 78:70; 89:3), Zerubbabel (Hag 2:23), and the prophets (Jer 7:25; 25:4; Amos 3:7; Zech 1:6), who each articulated God's revelation. By identifying himself with them, Paul is placing his apostleship on the same level, as a mouthpiece revealing God's truth.[55] This identity stands in contrast to his life prior to knowing God's grace, which was marked by disobedience, envy, and hatred (3:3). Beth Wilson also argues that Paul's willingness to identify his past failures and transformed status demonstrates a high level of self-awareness necessary for leadership.[56]

Embracing his new identity, Paul has been entrusted by God with the preaching of his word (1:3), and the purpose of his ministry is that God's people might grow in the knowledge of the truth that leads to godliness (ἐπίγνωσιν ἀληθείας τῆς κατ' εὐσέβειαν) so that they might gain eternal life (1:1–2).[57] The content of the truth is spelled out in 1:2–4, outlining God's eternal plan of salvation focused in Christ and made known through the gospel. Paul intends for a growing understanding of the truth to result in growing godliness; belief is to be seen in behaviour.[58] The expectation is that the integration of knowledge

---

52. Smith, *Pauline Communities*, 71–72; Knight, *Pastoral Epistles*, 311; Kelly, *Pastoral Epistles*, 242.
53. See the full list of imperatives in Yarbrough, *Timothy and Titus*, 505.
54. My translation. This is Paul's only use of δοῦλος θεοῦ in the NT to describe himself.
55. Wall and Steele, *1 & 2 Timothy and Titus*, 335.
56. Wilson, "Authentic Leadership," 205, 208.
57. Gourgues, *Lettres*, 354–55; Fee, *1 & 2 Timothy, Titus*, 168–69.
58. Akin, "Titus," 228.

and godliness is for all God's people (1:1), including Paul. Collectively this implies that Paul integrated a right understanding of God's mercy and grace with godly character, and humble and accurate self-perception of his identity.

The Church

Titus is directed to appoint elders in the churches across Crete (1:5), suggesting there would be consistency between what is expected of candidates for the position (1:6–9), and the churches they are drawn from. What we find is that the integration of right theology and godly behaviour in the lives of believers dominates chapters 2 and 3 of the letter.

The primary concern of 2:1–10 is that the teaching of sound doctrine (τῇ ὑγιαινούσῃ διδασκαλίᾳ, v. 1) will produce spiritual health (ὑγιαίνοντας τῇ πίστει, v. 2), showing itself in lives full of good deeds. The content of the doctrine is articulated in 2:11–14, with the use of *gar* (γὰρ) in verse 11 indicating that verses 11–14 provide the theological rationale for the behaviour of verses 1–10. Central to this doctrine is "the grace of God" (v. 11) which trains or educates (παιδεύουσα) believers to renounce ungodliness (ἀσέβειαν) and live godly lives (εὐσεβῶς ζήσωμεν) (v. 12). Paul has reconfigured the basis of *paideia* by grounding it in God's grace. Responding to God's grace, rather than seeking to acquire social status, becomes the motivation underpinning godly living. This is to show itself across the congregation, with 2:1–10 covering older men (v. 2), older women (v. 3), younger women (vv. 4–5), younger men (v. 6), and slaves and masters (vv. 9–10). The emphasis is on doing and teaching what is good (vv. 3, 5, 10) and being self-controlled (σώφρονας, vv. 2, 5–6). Sound doctrine will show itself in godly character as the grace of God educates and trains believers.[59] Flowing from this is the missional impact of the integrated lives of the congregation. Their grace-driven, godly lives ensure that the word of God (ὁ λόγος τοῦ θεοῦ) will not be maligned (vv. 5, 8) but will be made attractive (v. 10) to a watching world.[60] A sign of the healthy integration of theology and character will be the impact of the lives of believers on people outside the church.

---

59. Flichy, "Une Lecture de Tite 1,1–2,15," 128–29.
60. Wieland, "Grace Manifest," 9.

The integration of belief and behaviour for all believers continues to be seen in chapter 3. The use of *gar* (γὰρ) in verse 3 indicates that verses 3–8a provide the theological rationale for the behaviour of verses 1–2 and 8b–d, with the importance of this content further emphasized by its being called a faithful saying (Πιστὸς ὁ λόγος, v. 8a). At its heart is the saving action of God as Father, Son, and Spirit because of his mercy and grace. Paul's concern is that God's people will devote themselves to good works (vv. 1, 8, 14). This will show itself as believers submit to the civic authorities (v. 1) and are kind and peaceable with all people (vv. 2, 8).[61] A further indication of the healthy integration of theology and character is the congregation's support for missionaries. The church is to "make every effort to send Zenas the lawyer and Apollos on their way, and see that they lack nothing" (3:13).[62] "Sending them on their way" translates *propempō* (Πρόπεμπω), a technical term applied in the New Testament only to those who are involved in mission work.[63] Although verse 13 is directed to Titus, the connectives of verse 14 indicate that Titus is to involve all the believers.[64] Therefore, an aspect of the congregation's good works driven by sound doctrine is their involvement and ongoing support of missionaries, support that encompasses all that they need.

The integration of sound doctrine and godly behaviour expressed in the life of the churches on Crete is therefore an important theme in the letter of Titus. As such, it demonstrates a consistency between what was expected of potential elders and the churches they came from.

Signs of the Wrong Type of Integration

The letter to Titus also displays signs of a wrong type of integration in 1:10–16 and 3:9–11. In contrast to sound doctrine, there are people teaching what should not be taught (1:11). It would seem the content of this false teaching is Jewish myths (1:14) about genealogies and the law (3:9) coming especially from those emphasizing circumcision (1:10).[65] Paul regards their teaching

---

61. Herzer, "Kindness of God," 132.
62. Ζηνᾶν τὸν νομικὸν καὶ ⌜Ἀπολλῶν σπουδαίως πρόπεμψον, ἵνα μηδὲν αὐτοῖς λείπῃ.
63. Dickson, *Mission-Commitment*, 194–201.
64. Dickson, 201.
65. Schlarb, *Die gesunde Lehre*, 83.

as lies (1:12–13) and as a rejection of the truth (1:14). Their motivation for teaching what is false is unhealthy: it is for sordid gain (1:11). The impact of their teaching is also unhealthy. First, it is overturning or ruining complete households (1:11) and creating divisions within the congregation (3:10). Second, the false teaching has corrupted the minds and consciences of the false teachers themselves, rendering them incapable of good works but capable only of what is sinful (1:15–16; 3:11), and thus stands in complete contrast to the healthy effect of sound doctrine. The wrong type of integration is summarized in 1:16: "they profess to know God, but they deny him by their actions"; and the signs of "disease" include false teaching, wrong motives, corrupted consciences, and the inability to carry out good works.

Summary

Examining the letter of Titus supports the claim that integration in the LTT is made up of theology, skills, and character, and this can also be added to. Titus is to appoint overseers drawn from churches in which right theology is to be integrated with godly, ethical behaviour in the lives of all believers. The use of the stewardship metaphor highlights that the skills of leadership and teaching were also requirements for the overseers in addition to sound doctrine and godly character, and is reinforced by the same qualities being embodied in Titus. The pattern is broadened by Paul integrating identity and ministry with theology and godliness.

Integration and the Purpose of the Letter to Titus

The greeting (1:4) and ministry imperatives noted earlier suggest the letter is directed primarily to Titus as Paul's delegate, and the plural "you" (ὑμῶν) in the closing salutation (3:15) indicates that it is to be read to the congregation. The purpose of the letter is signalled by a combination of 1:5 and 3:14. Paul has entrusted Titus with the task of appointing elders among the churches in Crete and wants these congregations to be fruitful and productive in their good deeds and so effective in witness. Healthy doctrine is needed to produce godly lives in the face of teaching that is diseased, motivated by greed, and unable to produce good works. Gordon Fee describes Titus as "both *prophylactic* (serving to warn against false teachings) and *evangelistic* (serving to encourage behaviour that will be attractive to the world) in its thrust."[66]

Given that knowledge of the truth leads to godliness, Titus is to model the integration of healthy doctrine, godly living, and skilful teaching and leadership for the health of the congregation, and is to appoint elders who display the same qualities. Healthy, integrated leaders are needed for both the internal health of the congregation and its external witness to the world in both word and good deeds. Integration is tightly connected to the purpose of the letter.

Observations about Integration in the LTT

Having examined each of the LTT, what can we say about the content of integration?

First, the LTT support the claim that the content of integration involves theology, skills, and character, and this is seen in the lives of overseers, the "faithful people," Timothy, Titus, and Paul. Right "theology," according to the LTT, is the sound doctrine which brings salvation, grounded in the gospel of the historical life, death, and resurrection of Jesus Christ; "character" is ethical behaviour of godly living in keeping with the truth; and "skills" are those tasks (such as leadership and teaching) which are expected to be done with a high degree of competency.

Those who aspire to be overseers and deacons are to hold to the truth, be above reproach, and be able to teach and lead people (1 Tim 3:1–13), with the metaphor of the steward in Titus reinforcing the same idea. Similarly, the "faithful people" of 2 Timothy 2:2 are to be of good character, committed to the truth, and competent teachers. Timothy is to train himself in godliness, paying attention to his life so that he can set an example of righteous speech and action while he skilfully handles the word of truth, preaching the life-saving word in season and out of season. Titus is also to embody sound doctrine, godly character, and skilful teaching and leadership. Timothy and Titus also teach and model in such a way that those they teach are equipped, in turn, to teach others (2 Tim 2:2; Titus 2:3–4), thus indicating a high degree of skill. As Timothy and Titus integrate theology, skills, and character in their own

---

66. Fee, *1 & 2 Timothy, Titus*, 11.

lives, the expectation is that those they train up and appoint to ministries of teaching and leadership in the congregation will emulate their teaching and example. In this sense, Timothy and Titus are following the pattern of Paul, who integrated theology, skills, and godly character. Integration is thus found in the lives of overseers, the "faithful people," Timothy, Titus, and Paul, and as such, it confirms the claim that its content involves theology, skills, and character.

Second, the evidence of the letters reveals that in one sense, the content of integration in the LTT is "narrower" than originally suggested. The emphasis *in the churches* at Ephesus and Crete falls on the integration of theology and godly character but does not include skills, which is different from what is seen in the lives of overseers, the "faithful people," Timothy, Titus, and Paul. The household of God is to be well ordered, reflecting God's desire that people might be saved and come to a knowledge of the truth (1 Tim 2:3–4; 3:15–16). This is to be expressed in the public gathering (1 Tim 2:1–15) and in the honour and care they show for one another (1 Tim 5:1–6:2). All believers are to shun evil because they belong to the Lord (2 Tim 2:19). The grace of God that saves people is the same grace that trains and educates the church to live godly lives, transforming them from their previous malicious behaviour so they can devote themselves to good deeds (Titus 2:11–12; 3:3–8). At the congregational level, indeed for all believers, sound theology and godly character are integrated. This is emphasized by the contrast with false teaching and its effects found throughout the LTT. Jouette Bassler sums up by saying, "A fundamental presupposition throughout these letters is that there is an indissoluble connection between beliefs and behaviour, between doctrine and ethics. Stated simply – and repeatedly – sound teaching and sound behaviour go hand in hand."[67]

Third, the LTT also demonstrate that what is integrated is "broader" than originally thought, and includes identity, ministry, and suffering. According to the LTT, "identity" is one's standing before God based on the saving work of Christ; "ministry" involves serving God's saving purposes for this world; and "suffering" is enduring hardship for the sake of the truth of the gospel. In addition to theology, skills, and character, integration for Paul includes his identity (e.g. 1 Tim 1:12–17; 2 Tim 1:8, 11), self-perception (Titus 3:3–8),

---

67. Bassler, *1 Timothy, 2 Timothy, Titus*, 34.

hard work in ministry (1 Tim 4:9–10), and the conduct of his ministry (1 Tim 1:20; 2 Tim 4:17). Each of these relates to Paul's theology and is seen in his behaviour. In a similar vein, Timothy is a "man of God" who teaches and leads with authority using the Scriptures. All believers are the elect and belong to God and his household. Whether individually or corporately, identity reflects a theological understanding and is shown in godly living.

The letter of 2 Timothy makes a particular contribution to the discussion by including suffering as part of integration. All believers will be persecuted for seeking to live a godly life (2 Tim 3:12). This requires faithful perseverance (2:10–13), knowing the eschatological judge will reward all who do so (4:8). In addition, the LTT point to Paul, Timothy, Titus, and those in leadership positions, such as overseers, facing opposition and difficulty because they are faithful to the content of the gospel and its proclamation. Being a handler of God's word brings with it an extra dimension of suffering on top of suffering for living a godly life. This is to be endured by God's power (2 Tim 1:8), knowing that those who do so will reign with Christ Jesus (2 Tim 2:12).

Having examined what is integrated in the LTT, the next chapter will focus on how this is done: the process of integration.

Discussion Questions

1. "'Entrusting' involved equipping the 'faithful people' in such a way that they in turn would be able to teach others." What are the implications of this for theological education?

2. Second Timothy points to suffering being part of integration. How might this be incorporated in your context?

3. The LTT demonstrate that there is a wrong type of integration. What might the wrong type of integration look like in your situation? How do you guard against it?

4. The LTT highlight that the emphasis in the churches falls on integrating theology and godly character, and in addition, leaders require skills. What are the implications of this for theological education in your context?

5

The Process of Integration in the Letters to Timothy and Titus

*H*ow have you been shaped as a person, disciple of Jesus, and servant of the word? Most of us would quickly identify the powerful influence our family has had in our formation, both negatively and positively. One of my childhood memories I have come to cherish is, as a little boy, walking into my parents' bedroom to find my father on his knees praying for us, his family. When I became a father many years later, that memory was a powerful example to draw upon.

There are many other ways in which we are shaped and moulded. For example, it could be sitting under faithful preaching week by week, or the care you received from people in your church when life was particularly difficult for you. Perhaps it has been the willingness of your church pastor or denominational leader to suffer for Jesus as they have been locked up or had their house burnt. Or perhaps you have had the opportunity to interact with people from other parts of the world, and this has given you fresh eyes through which to see your home culture. There are many, many ways we are shaped; and under God's good, gracious, and sovereign hand, none of them are wasted.

In the previous two chapters we have established that integration in the LTT involves theology, skills, character, identity, ministry, and suffering. We turn now to examine the factors which contribute to the overall process of integration in the LTT: *how* does integration happen? We noted earlier in the book that the LTT were not written to theological education institutions but to individuals exercising ministry in a church context, and therefore how integration occurs both corporately in churches and in individuals like Timothy and Titus needs to be taken into consideration. Students entering theological education institutions have already been shaped by their experience of church life, so the healthier that experience, the more likely it is that integration is taking place. Therefore, examining the LTT for how integration takes place in churches, as well as for individuals, is relevant to understanding integration in theological education.

This chapter presents evidence of eleven contexts that contribute to the process of integration in the LTT. The first eight contexts are common to the process of integration that occurs both in the church and in individuals. Integration takes place in a matrix of relationally rich environments including households, church, and being part of global mission. Prayer, shared ministry experience, and modelling are important as Paul provided an example of life and ministry to Timothy and Titus, and they in turn were to be models for the overseers, "faithful people," and church. Instruction and contextualization are also contexts that contribute to integration. A further three contexts are focused on individuals such as Timothy, Titus, and the "faithful people," with the additional contexts being relationship with Paul, personal responsibility, and the training of people to train others. The chapter takes a synthetic approach, recognizing features common to the LTT; where practices are specific to a particular letter, these are also noted.

Contexts Contributing to the Process of Integration
Household

The first context contributing to the process of integration is the households within the church. Providing for the household, and especially for those really in need, is evidence of putting godliness into practice, for this pleases God (1 Tim 5:3–8). Similarly, the way in which wives love their husbands and children shows that they are practising the good teaching in which they have been trained (Titus 2:3–5). In addition, the manner in which masters and their slaves relate to one another provides the opportunity to demonstrate the integration of belief and behaviour so that God's name may be honoured (1 Tim 6:1–2; Titus 2:9–10).

The foundational context in which overseers and deacons integrate theology, skills, and character is their own households. In this context they hold to the truth and display godly character and leadership of people (1 Tim 3:1–13; Titus 1:6–9).[1] The importance of the domestic context is emphasized by 1 Timothy 3:5: "If anyone does not know how to manage his own family, how can he take care of God's church?" (NIV). The household is also presented in 2 Timothy as a setting in which integration occurred for Timothy. Timothy had known the Scriptures from infancy (2 Tim 3:15) through the faith of his grandmother Lois and mother Eunice (2 Tim 1:5), and their teaching and example had contributed to his understanding of God's word and its application in his life. The household was a significant relational context in which integration took place.

Church

The second context contributing to the process of integration is the churches at Ephesus and Crete (1 Tim 1:3; 3:14–15; 2 Tim 1:18; 4:12; Titus 1:5).[2] Integration did not occur in isolation, nor just in a master–disciple type relationship between Timothy and Titus and Paul; the LTT present the local congregation as the major context in which integration happens, and this reflects the centrality of the church in God's plans.[3] The church is God's household, holding up and holding out the truth, and certain behaviours are expected (1 Tim 3:15).[4] This contributes to defining and reinforcing the identity of those involved, based on who they are in relation to God through Christ (1 Tim 3:16; 2 Tim 2:10; Titus 3:7). The church is also God's agent of mission, as it prays for the society (1 Tim 2:1–3) and promotes the faith by word and deed (1 Tim 5:7–8; Titus 2:5, 8), even if this means suffering (2 Tim 3:12). Thus, theology, identity, character, ministry, and suffering are integrated in the church. Given the centrality of the church to God's plans, it is not surprising it provides such an important context for integration.

---

1. Adams, "Shape of the Pauline Churches," 133.
2. Although there is overlap between households and churches, 1 Tim 3:5 strongly suggests there is a distinction between them.
3. Merkle, "Ecclesiology in the Pastoral Epistles," 198.
4. Brox, *Die Pastoralbriefe*, 156.

Having demonstrated the right qualities domestically, church provides another communal context for integration in the lives of overseers, deacons, and "faithful people." Before deacons can serve, they are to be tested (1 Tim 3:10). Elders who lead the church well are to be treated with honour and respect, especially those who handle the word of God (presuming they do this faithfully and skilfully, 1 Tim 5:17). Their sound teaching nourishes and protects the congregation and the households who constitute it (Titus 1:9–11), and the "faithful people" are to pass on the truth among other people. Overseers, deacons, and "faithful people" live and exercise ministry in the relational network of the church.

The church is the setting in which Timothy had been gifted as the elders laid hands on him (1 Tim 4:14), and his growth in godliness and ministry is to be observable in the congregation (1 Tim 4:15). He is to keep reminding the church of the truth (2 Tim 2:14) and gently instruct his opponents, with the aim of bringing them to repentance (2 Tim 2:25–26). Like Timothy, Titus is ministering in local church settings in the towns of Crete (Titus 1:5). He serves among "our people" (NIV; οἱ ἡμέτεροι, Titus 3:14), which includes men and women, older and younger, slaves and masters (Titus 2:1–10).

A dimension of church life that facilitates integration for all parties (the church, overseers, deacons, "faithful people," Timothy, and Titus) is mutual accountability. The overseers are publicly accountable to the church, but any accusations must be substantiated (1 Tim 5:19–20). Timothy is to keep integrating theology, skills, and character in such a way that the church may see his growth and development (1 Tim 4:15). Mutual accountability is enabled by Paul's letters as they are addressed to Timothy and Titus, and publicly read (1 Tim 6:21; 2 Tim 4:22; Titus 3:15) so that everyone hears and knows what is expected for life together in the household of God (1 Tim 3:15).

Global Mission

The third context promoting the process of integration is the involvement of the church in global mission. The church in Crete is to "make every effort to send Zenas the lawyer and Apollos on their way, and see that they lack nothing" (Titus 3:13), and we noted in the previous chapter that "sending them on their way" translates *propempō* (Πρόπεμπω), a technical term applied in the New

Testament only to those who are involved in mission work.[5] Involvement in global mission is an expression of the church integrating their good works of ministry and sound doctrine.

Second Timothy 4:9–22 also makes both the church at Ephesus and Timothy and Titus aware that they are part of global mission. Paul reports on the movements and ministries of other believers, as well as of those who oppose the gospel. His commitment to global mission stems from the task entrusted to him by the Lord, that all the Gentiles might hear the gospel message (v. 17; Acts 9:15), and reflects God's desire that all might be saved (1 Tim 2:4). Titus has gone to Dalmatia, and Timothy is to come to Paul, indicating they have integrated the same gospel message with a behavioural commitment to its proclamation.

Example

Personal example is the fourth context contributing to the process of integration. Timothy's life is to be an example that complements his teaching by modelling for the church what a godly life looks like (1 Tim 4:12); doctrinal belief and character are integrated and demonstrated for the church.[6] Timothy will also provide an example to the overseers and deacons as he has nothing to do with false teaching and its effects (1 Tim 4:7; 6:20).[7] Instead, Timothy is to guard the gospel (1 Tim 6:20).[8] If the overseers and deacons are to be people who "keep hold of the deep truths of the faith" (1 Tim 3:9 NIV), they will see it modelled by Timothy. Proactively, Timothy is to preach the word regardless of circumstances (2 Tim 4:2–5) and thus model faithful proclamation to "faithful people" and the congregation. Titus is also to be a model for the elders and the whole congregation. His example must cover the whole of life (περὶ πάντα) as well as the content and manner of his teaching (Titus 2:7–8), thus demonstrating integration.

---

5. Dickson, *Mission-Commitment*, 194–201.
6. Fiore says that, by stressing Timothy's character, 1 Tim 4:12 diminishes the word; however, v. 13 undermines such a claim. Fiore, *Function of Personal Example*, 209.
7. Redalié and O'Donnell both argue that the structure of 1 Timothy places the example of Timothy's life and doctrine at its centre. Redalié, "'Sois un modèle,'" 90–92; O'Donnell, "Rhetorical Strategy," 466–67.
8. Towner, *Letters to Timothy and Titus*, 431.

In 1 Timothy 1:15–17, Paul holds himself up as the chief example of a sinner who has been shown grace and mercy by Christ Jesus to the glory of God. Knowing this grace and mercy shapes Paul's identity and behaviour as they are integrated. The purpose of his example is to show that if God could save him, then he can save anyone. The effect in the flow of 1:3–20 is to remind Timothy of the centrality of grace to the gospel, in contrast to the mishandling of the law by the opponents (1:7).

Paul's personal example is a strong feature of 2 Timothy. Based on his own suffering as a prisoner for the gospel, Paul calls on Timothy to follow his example (2 Tim 1:8–12). Paul's "teaching includes life practice as well and is verified by that practice."[9] Similarly, Paul exhorts Timothy to persevere in faithfulness to the Scriptures, even in the face of persecution, because of what Paul has done (2 Tim 3:10–14). The use of *parēkolouthēsas* (παρηκολούθησάς, 3:10) indicates that Timothy previously followed the example of Paul as a disciple would his master, so this section acts as a call to renewed commitment to imitating his way of life and ministry.[10] Given his track record, Paul can claim he has remained faithful and looks forward to his eternal reward, and he uses his example to encourage all believers to do the same (2 Tim 4:6–8). Paul also hints at his example of contented living in 1 Timothy 6:6–7. Finally, Paul provides an example of his approach to ministry in his dealing with Hymenaeus and Alexander (1 Tim 1:20). He will not put up with them destroying the faith, and yet he also puts them in a position in which they may learn and change. Theology, character, identity, ministry, and suffering are integrated in Paul's life.

Victor Copan has demonstrated that in the ancient world the imitation of a model was found in the relational spheres of parent–child, teacher–student, and leader–people.[11] He argues that Paul combines the roles of parent, teacher, and leader in providing a model for his co-workers and other believers, a point endorsed by the LTT.[12] Paul's example provides a model to be copied by his

---

9. Fiore, *Personal Example*, 205. Donelson says Paul embodies gospel truths, but takes it a step further to claim that Paul "becomes part of the content of the gospel." This contradicts the christological focus of 1:9–12 and 2:8–13. Donelson, "Studying Paul," 726–27.
10. Collins, *Timothy and Titus*, 255; Gloer, *1 & 2 Timothy–Titus*, 280; Ngewa, *1 & 2 Timothy and Titus*, 279.
11. Copan, *Saint Paul*, 40–71.
12. Copan, 71. Copan does not interact with the LTT.

delegates. He has guarded and proclaimed the gospel that was entrusted to him. His teaching, character, and perseverance in the face of suffering are known and embody what an integrated minister looks like in practice.

Instruction

Instruction is the fifth context contributing to the process of integration. Integration in the church is fostered by the overseers, deacons, and whole congregation receiving instruction through Timothy and Titus. Instruction can be regarded as an umbrella term that covers public and personal settings and includes preaching, teaching, training, and the passing on of sound doctrine and its implications for godly behaviour.

Integration is fostered by public instruction. Timothy is to be dedicated to the public reading of Scripture and preaching and teaching (τῇ ἀναγνώσει, τῇ παρακλήσει, τῇ διδασκαλίᾳ, 1 Tim 4:13), with the expectation that he will be teaching all that Paul has instructed and taught him so that the congregation can live in keeping with their identity as God's household (1 Tim 3:15; 4:6, 11). The overseers, deacons, and the whole church will know what the truth is and how to behave because Timothy publicly instructs them.

Likewise, in 2 Timothy 4:2 Timothy is directed to "preach the word" (NIV; κήρυξον τὸν λόγον) in all circumstances. This includes the way he goes about the task – carefully and with great patience and gentleness (2 Tim 2:25; 4:2). It is only the sound doctrine Timothy offers the church that can produce spiritual health, in contrast to the powerlessness of false teaching that lacks the truth (2 Tim 3:1–7). The integration of teaching and godly character will require patient and careful instruction in the truth.

Integration is also fostered by the "training" Timothy will conduct among the church. Smith highlights that in the ancient world, *didaskō* ("teaching," διδάσκω) involved not only the passing on of information but also the acquisition of skill, and learning from the personal example of the teacher.[13] In many cases in the LTT *didaskō* refers to "the teaching" or "doctrine" (e.g. 1 Tim 1:10; 4:1; 4:6; 2 Tim 3:10; 4:3; Titus 1:9; 2:1; 2:10) but at other points it could be best thought of as referring to "training." In 1 Timothy 4:11 and 6:2, Paul directs Timothy to "teach [δίδασκε] these things" (NIV). The context of both

---

13. Smith, *Pauline Communities*, 54.

passages demonstrates that Timothy is to teach the truth of God's word and a lifestyle of godliness within the church, covering issues such as marriage, what they eat, physical exercise, material support for the needy, support of church leadership, church discipline, and the working relationship between slaves and masters. This suggests that "teaching" is more than the communication of doctrinal truths (although it certainly includes this); it also involves training the church in the lifestyle and behavioural patterns that flow from the truth.[14]

In turn, the overseers are to faithfully instruct the church through their preaching and teaching (1 Tim 3:2; 5:17). The distinction 1 Timothy 5:17 makes between preaching and teaching (λόγῳ καὶ διδασκαλίᾳ) suggests that their teaching may have involved not just the public proclamation of God's word but also the training of believers in how to obey that word in their circumstances. Given that 1 Timothy 5:17 occurs in a lengthy section (1 Tim 5:1–6:2) covering the behavioural implications of sound doctrine for the church, this may well be the case. Training will help the church integrate what they believe and how they live.

In 2 Timothy 3:16, Paul urges Timothy to keep using the Scriptures in his ministry because they are

> useful for teaching [*didaskalian*, διδασκαλίαν],
>   rebuking,
>   correcting
> and training [*paideian*, παιδείαν] in righteousness. (NIV)

The chiasm of the verse highlights the parallel between teaching and training, suggesting they were closely related activities, and links together instruction in doctrine with righteous living.[15] As Timothy seeks to encourage believers to live godly lives in Christ Jesus (2 Tim 3:12) in the face of false teaching and persecution, they will need to be trained by him using the Scriptures. A similar parallel is found in Titus 2:3–4 in which the older women are to "teach what is good" (καλοδιδασκάλους) and "train [σωφρονίζωσι] the young women," (ESV) with *sōphronizōsi* meaning to bring them to their senses through the

---

14. Neudorfer says personal care is involved but the emphasis of "teaching" falls on public proclamation. Neudorfer, *Der erste Brief*, 180.

15. Spicq, *Les Épîtres pastorales*, 2.788–89; Marshall, *Pastoral Epistles*, 795; Mounce, *Pastoral Epistles*, 570.

imparting of practical wisdom.[16] The context suggests that "teaching what is good" is focused on living out godly behaviour in everyday circumstances (Titus 2:4–5) motivated by God's grace (Titus 2:11–12), and this occurs through the modelling and personal instruction of the older women.[17]

Titus 2:1–15 is framed by Paul's command that Titus must teach (λάλει, vv. 1, 15) and reinforced by the call to encourage and rebuke (v. 15). The verb *laleō* refers to ordinary, everyday speech rather than formal conversation.[18] When coupled with the reference to the manner and content of Titus's teaching (τῇ διδασκαλίᾳ, v. 7), it suggests that he is involved in training the various groups within the congregation through ongoing conversations. By the teaching of sound doctrine (2:1), the grace of God trains believers to say "no" to worldly passions and "yes" to godliness (2:12), helping them to integrate belief and behaviour. Titus is to remind the church about how to behave (3:1), and the basis of this behaviour, the trustworthy saying of 3:3–7, is something that Titus is to stress or insist upon (διαβεβαιοῦσθαι, 3:8). For the church to integrate doctrine and ethics will require sound training and teaching from Titus. This is to be replicated by the overseers appointed by Titus as they instruct the church in sound doctrine (1:9).

Instruction also involves the process of entrusting the gospel to the "faithful people" of 2 Timothy 2:2. Just as Paul had entrusted (παρατίθεμαί, 1 Tim 1:18) Timothy with the task of not allowing false doctrine, so now Timothy is to entrust (παράθου) "faithful people" with the apostolic gospel he has heard from Paul. This involves public teaching and proclamation, as indicated by the presence of witnesses. So too, the "faithful people" are to listen to Timothy as he instructs them and entrusts them with the gospel.

Paul's instruction of Timothy and Titus contributes to their integration of theology, skills, character, identity, ministry, and suffering. Paul writes each of the LTT as an apostle of Jesus Christ (1 Tim 1:1; 2 Tim 1:1, 11; Titus 1:1), and as we saw in chapter 4, he identifies himself with those in the Old Testament who articulated God's revelation, thus placing his apostleship on the same

---

16. Perkins, *Pastoral Letters*, 261; Fee, *1 & 2 Timothy, Titus*, 187.
17. Akin, "Titus," 259.
18. Yarbrough, *Timothy and Titus*, 507, 533–34; Hutson, *Timothy and Titus*, 228. Knight and Mounce suggest that *laleō* is used as a synonym for *didaskō*. See Knight, *Pastoral Epistles*, 305; Mounce, *Pastoral Epistles*, 408.

level, as a mouthpiece revealing God's truth (Titus 1:1–3).[19] Instruction had previously happened face to face as they heard Paul's explanations (1 Tim 1:3; 2 Tim 1:4, 13; 2:2; Titus 1:5), but now, in his absence, the letters function as his instructions to them, conveying his apostolic presence and authority.[20]

Throughout 1 Timothy, Paul gives a range of commands (1:3, 18; 4:11; 5:7, 21; 6:17), exhortations (1:3; 2:1), and imperatives (e.g. 4:7, 11, 12, 13, 14, 15, 16) designed to instruct Timothy in how he and the church should act as God's household and the rationale behind it. The repeated use of second-person imperatives directed at Timothy indicates the importance and extent of Paul's desire to teach and guide Timothy.

Similarly, in 2 Timothy Paul uses imperatives to command Timothy to guard the truth (1:14), entrust it to others (2:2), remember Jesus (2:8), and avoid godless people and what they say (2:16, 23; 3:5). These instructions come to a climax in the final, solemn charge of 4:1–5 in which Timothy is to "preach the word" (4:2 NIV). This functions as a heading for the other imperatives: to preach the word persistently by convincing, rebuking, and encouraging (4:2).[21] Further commands to be sober, endure, evangelize, and continue in ministry follow in verse 5.

In the letter to Titus, Paul reinforces his previous directives (Titus 1:5); Titus is to carry on with what he has been told. Paul directs Titus with eleven imperatives through the letter which are focused on his task of teaching, rebuking, and exhorting the believers (e.g. 1:13; 2:1, 6, 15; 3:10).[22] In Titus 2:1, the placement of "you" at the beginning of the sentence emphasizes what Paul is directing Titus to do (i.e. teach sound doctrine).[23] In Titus 3:8, Paul wants (βούλομαί) Titus to insist on the content of the trustworthy saying (3:3–7). *Boulomai* is also used in 1 Timothy 2:8 and 5:7 and carries the weight of an apostolic instruction.[24]

---

19. See section on "Paul" under "2 Timothy," in chapter 4 above.
20. Stirewalt Jr., *Paul the Letter Writer*, 120; Johnson, *Letters to Timothy*, 141.
21. Griffiths, *Preaching in the New Testament*, 56–57.
22. See the table in Yarbrough, *Timothy and Titus*, 505.
23. Akin, "Titus," 255.
24. Knight, *Pastoral Epistles*, 351; Fiore, *Pastoral Epistles*, 12, 64. However, Mounce, *Pastoral Epistles*, 452, does not think it is this forceful.

A focal point of instruction is the use of Scripture. Timothy is to be committed to "the reading, the preaching, the teaching" (τῇ ἀναγνώσει, τῇ παρακλήσει, τῇ διδασκαλίᾳ, 1 Tim 4:13, my translation) as the congregation gathers. For a reading to take place requires a text. In 2 Timothy 3:15–16, Paul urges Timothy to keep making use of the Scriptures to grow in godliness and be equipped for all that God wants him to do. Timothy is to make use of authoritative texts for his own benefit and for the benefit of the church, for using these texts will contribute to the integration of life and godliness. Generally, it is thought that this was an adaptation of the synagogue practice of reading the Hebrew scriptures (OT), followed by an explanation of it.[25] Timothy Swinson takes this further, though, arguing that, because the content of "the preaching" and "the teaching" refers to the apostolic gospel in 1 Timothy, "the reading" (τῇ ἀναγνώσει) must include some gospel content as well as the Old Testament. Based on the quotation in 1 Timothy 5:18 that mirrors Luke 10:7, Swinson says this content is Luke's gospel.[26] Similarly, in 2 Timothy 3:14–17, he argues that "what you have learned and . . . believed" (οἷς ἔμαθες καὶ ἐπιστώθης, v. 14) refers to the gospel, and "the Holy Scriptures" (NIV; ἱερὰ γράμματα, v. 15) refers to the Old Testament. Together, they make "all scripture" (πᾶσα γραφὴ, v. 16).[27]

Swinson presents a plausible argument that a version of Luke's gospel may have been in circulation, but this must not be seen in isolation from other avenues of information about the gospel tradition. As Towner highlights, 2 Corinthians 7:8; Colossians 4:16; 1 Thessalonians 5:27; and 2 Thessalonians 3:14 point to the distribution of authoritative Pauline letters.[28] Timothy may have used 2 Corinthians, Philippians, Colossians, and 1 and 2 Thessalonians, of which he was joint author. In addition, when Paul made use of a text, his practice was to reason from the Old Testament scriptures (Acts 16:16–48; 17:2, 11; 28:23). While Swinson's scenario is possible, it may only be part of the whole story. What can be said more confidently (even if generally) is that at a

---

25. Witherington, *Letters and Homilies*, 258; Quinn and Wacker, *Letters to Timothy*, 390–91.
26. Swinson, *What Is Scripture?*, 101–2; Wolfe, "Sagacious Use of Scripture," 211–16. Hultgren regards "the Scriptures" as only referring to the OT. See Hultgren, "Pastoral Epistles," 372–90, especially pp. 384–88.
27. Swinson, *What Is Scripture?*, 146–54.
28. Towner, *Letters to Timothy and Titus*, 317.

minimum the Old Testament was used, and most likely with a combination of various early New Testament texts. Integration involved the use of authoritative texts in the instruction of others.

Instruction is an important context contributing to integration. It occurred publicly and in personal conversations and mentoring settings, and included preaching, teaching, training, and the passing on of sound doctrine and its implications for godly behaviour, identity, ministry, and willingness to suffer. Through his letters, Paul continues to reinforce to Timothy and Titus the gospel message and its implications for godly living and ministry, and they in turn are to instruct the overseers, deacons, "faithful people," and church using authoritative texts.

Contextualization

Related to instructing the church and Timothy and Titus is contextualization, the sixth context that contributes to the process of integration. Paul's instructions are contextualized instructions which can be broadly grouped under the headings of contextualized theology and contextualized behaviour.

Paul expressed theology in contextualized terms. For example, God is described as "Saviour" (1 Tim 1:1; 2:3; 4:10; Titus 1:3; 2:10; 3:4), as is Jesus (2 Tim 1:10; Titus 1:4; 2:13; 3:6). As well as referring to a being found in the Old Testament, the term was previously used for Greek heroes and gods, and in the first century applied to the Roman emperor.[29] It spoke of the emperor's benevolence and power, his acting for his subjects who were not able to help themselves. Towner says "the decision to adapt this religiously-politically loaded language for Christian proclamation reveals the intention of each of the letters, to one degree or another, to take the dialogue with the culture of the day to another level."[30]

Another prominent example is the use of the term "godliness" (εὐσεβείᾳ).[31] *Eusebeia* was a mainstream concept in Graeco-Roman culture involving a person's obligations to the gods, his or her family, and the state, in order that the

---

29. E.g. *IG 2.1.902*; *IG 2.1.903*; *IG 2.3.4.10*; *IEph 251*; Towner, "Christology," 223; Belleville, "Pseudonymity of the Pastoral Epistles," 241–42.
30. Towner, "Christology," 226.
31. 1 Tim 2:2; 3:16; 4:7–8; 6:3, 5–6, 11; 2 Tim 3:5; Titus 1:1.

person might be honoured as a good citizen.³² However, in the LTT godliness is grounded in God's plan of salvation focused in Christ (1 Tim 2:2; 3:16; Titus 1:1), offering life now and into eternity (1 Tim 4:8; Titus 1:1), and is not to be a means of making money (1 Tim 6:5–6).³³ "The author of the Pastorals represents the *ekklēsia* as civilized and loyal imperial subjects who embody *pietas* – the very virtue that made Rome great – while redefining the contents of this virtue around their devotion to Christ."³⁴ In addition, the vocabulary of "appearing" (ἐπιφάνεια) is found in each of the LTT, which is a shift from the language of *parousia* (παρουσία) used in other parts of the New Testament (e.g. Matt 24:3, 27, 37, 39; 1 Cor 15:23; 1 Thess 2:19; 3:13; 4:15; 5:23; Jas 5:7–8).³⁵ In the ancient world *epiphaneia* was used to describe the appearance of a god or even the emperor.³⁶ In 2 Timothy 1:10 and Titus 2:11 and 3:4 it refers to the first appearing of Jesus, and in 1 Timothy 6:14; 2 Timothy 4:1, 8; and Titus 2:13 it refers to his appearance at the eschaton.³⁷ Paul has taken a term that has currency in the culture and given it new christological content.³⁸

"Saviour," "godliness," and "appearing" are three examples of terms that had contemporary currency in Graeco-Roman culture that Paul adapted and filled with fresh Christian content. In other words, he has contextualized Christian theology. Trebilco argues that Paul's choice of language, such as the examples above, was motivated by a desire to communicate well with his readers so his message would be better understood by unbelievers.³⁹ This missional strategy reflects God's desire that people come to a knowledge of the truth and be transformed by his grace. In effect, contextualization is a skill that

---

32. Hoklotubbe, *Civilized Piety*, 6.
33. Hoklotubbe, *Civilized Piety*, 130.
34. Hoklotubbe, 145. *Pietas* is the Latin equivalent of the Greek term *eusebeia*.
35. 1 Tim 6:14; 2 Tim 1:10; 4:1, 8; Titus 2:11, 13; 3:4.
36. E.g. *IEph 251*; *IEph 27*; Lau, *Manifest in Flesh*, 179–225.
37. Van Houwelingen argues all the references in 2 Timothy refer to Christ's first coming, but see the response from Manomi. Van Houwelingen, "Meaning of Ἐπιφάνεια"; Manomi, "Salvific, Ethical, and Consummative."
38. Stettler, *Die Christologie der Pastoralbriefe*, 311; Collins, "From Πλρουσιλ to Επιθλνειλ," 296–98.
39. Trebilco, *Early Christians*, 374; Lau, *Manifest in Flesh*, 224; Ho, "Mission in the Pastoral Epistles," 265.

seeks to integrate theology, Christian living, and ministry in ways that are understandable to those listening.

The LTT also provide examples of contextualized behaviour. The leaders chosen for the congregation are to be above reproach and have a good reputation with those outside the church (1 Tim 3:7). In 1 Timothy 5:1–6:2, widows are to be cared for, for this pleases God (5:4), and so the church's witness to a watching world will not be undermined (5:7–8). Similarly, the younger widows are counselled to remarry in order to not be caught up in the effects of false teaching resulting in ungodliness and the faith being slandered (5:11–14). Slaves are to honour their masters so that the teaching about God and his character is not maligned (6:1–2), a theme that is repeated in Titus 2:9. Indeed, all the believers in Crete are to live in obedience to the civic leaders by doing what is good (Titus 3:1–2) so that God is honoured. A clear theme that runs through these examples is the concern for the reputation of God and his people in the eyes of the broader society. This reflects God's plan of salvation in which he uses his church for the mission of reaching the world for Christ. Ho says, "The 'good witness' motif is prominent in these letters. This has been seen to be inextricably bound to the gospel. In other words, the PE teaches that authentic Christian faith should reflect a lifestyle that witnesses positively for furthering the gospel."[40] Contextualization promotes the integration of right theology, godly living, identity as God's people, and ministry to the rest of society.

The contextualized behaviour presented in the LTT has been criticized for adopting the social conventions of its day. Dibelius and Conzelmann's assessment that the LTT had settled for a Christian citizenship that would not upset the society has proved influential.[41] Korinna Zamfir says,

> The PE visibly share the essential values of contemporary society, including elements of an honour and shame mentality, values that they seek to inculcate to members of the *ekklēsia* . . . In a sense the *ekklēsia* becomes a society in society, a *polis* within the *polis*, in line with the norms of honourable behaviour. This focus on

---

40. Ho, 265.
41. Dibelius and Conzelmann, *Pastoral Epistles*, 39–41; see Towner, *Goal of Our Instruction*, 9–16.

honour and shame receives a slim theological motivation, through
the few references to God and Christ.⁴²

While the LTT reflect some of the values of the surrounding society, presenting this as a wholesale and uncritical adoption is an exaggeration. Trebilco points to three areas which suggest the conscious rejection of the surrounding culture.⁴³ First, the use of contemporary terms undermined claims that "godliness" involved loyalty to the emperor as the "Saviour" who had "appeared" for the benefit of his people, as these appellations were now Christocentric for believers. Second, the LTT display a different attitude to wealth from that of society (1 Tim 6). Third, honour is given in the Christian community to real widows, elders, and the masters of Christian slaves, standing in contrast to society's practice of honouring the rich. To this list can be added the willingness to suffer for the gospel and for living a godly life (2 Tim 1:8, 12; 3:12) that is countercultural to the surrounding society.

In instructing the church and Timothy and Titus, Paul contextualizes theology and behaviour and this promotes the integration of theology, godly character, identity, ministry, and suffering. Given the imperatives that Paul uses, it is not unreasonable to say that he expects them to also contextualize their theology, life, and ministry.

Prayer

Prayer is the seventh context contributing to the process of integration. Although prayer is not mentioned in the letter to Titus, it is touched upon in the letters to Timothy. As part of the church knowing how to act as the household of God, Paul instructs Timothy that the congregation is to pray (1 Tim 2:1), motivated by God's desire that people be saved (1 Tim 2:3–6).⁴⁴ The men are to take the initiative and set the example in prayer in godliness and content (1 Tim 2:8). It is reasonable to assume that the overseers and deacons were among those leading these prayers, and thus prayer is a means of them integrating godly character and theology. In a similar vein, prayer is

---

42. Zamfir, *Men and Women*, 103, 126–27.
43. Trebilco, *Early Christians*, 379–83.
44. Neudorfer says the primacy of prayer is suggested by its position in these intructions. Neudorfer, *Der erste Brief*, 103–5; Oberlinner, *Die Pastoralbriefe*, 1.66.

an expression of Timothy integrating godly behaviour and right theology. In contrast to the false teachers who order people to abstain from eating certain foods (1 Tim 4:3), Timothy is to teach the church that what God created is good and is to be accepted with prayers of thanksgiving (1 Tim 4:4–6).

Paul's digression about God's grace extended to him in Christ is a prayer of thanksgiving that concludes by praising and glorifying God (1 Tim 1:17). His prayer demonstrates that the theology of the gospel he has just explained is not simply something to which he gives intellectual assent but has profoundly altered his self-understanding. Theology is integrated with personal identity and expressed in prayerful praise of God. In 1 Timothy 6:15–16, Paul praises and glorifies God for his sovereign and eternal rule, understanding that, because of God's sovereignty, the Lord Jesus will return at a time of God's choosing. On this basis, Paul exhorts Timothy to remain steadfast in faith and godliness, following through on all that Paul has taught him (1 Tim 6:11–14). Paul's prayer of praise integrates eschatology with the life of faithful ministry. Paul is also thankful to God for Timothy's faith (2 Tim 1:3–7). His constant prayers for him are not just an expression of their deep friendship but also demonstrate Paul's commitment to Timothy's ministry.

Shared Ministry Experience

The eighth context contributing to the process of integration is shared ministry experience. Titus is directed by Paul to appoint elders for the churches in Crete (Titus 1:5) who will teach and encourage people through sound doctrine and refute those who oppose it (Titus 1:9). It was noted in the previous chapter that these activities parallel what Titus is to do, as he teaches, encourages (Titus 2:1, 15), and reminds (Titus 3:1) the congregation of sound doctrine and its behavioural implications. Given the overlap of activities, it is likely that there was some shared ministry experience between Titus and the overseers. A similar observation can be made for Timothy and the overseers and "faithful people," as each exercises a teaching ministry (e.g. 1 Tim 3:2; 4:13; 2 Tim 2:2, 14, 24).

A feature of 2 Timothy is the indications of shared ministry experience between Paul and Timothy. Paul's reminder (ἀναμιμνῄσκω, 1:6) to Timothy implies something they are both aware of from past experience that is to now have effect in the present.⁴⁵ Verse 6 indicates that their shared history goes back to the beginning of Timothy's faith when God's Spirit was confirmed in him.⁴⁶ We have already noted that Timothy heard the pattern of sound teaching from Paul (2 Tim 1:13) and was on hand as Paul explained it to many others (2 Tim 2:2). Now Paul urges Timothy to once again share in the experience of ministry by joining him in suffering for the gospel (2 Tim 1:8; 2:3). Titus 1:5 indicates that Titus had also previously been involved in ministry with Paul, as we see in 2 Corinthians and Galatians (e.g. 2 Cor 8:23; Gal 2:1–14).

The shared experience of ministry allows Paul, Timothy, Titus, overseers, and "faithful people" to demonstrate their commitment to God's truth and godly behaviour through use of their skills and gifts and their willingness to suffer for the gospel. It is motivated by a theological understanding of God's plans to rescue sinners and redeem a people for himself who will live lives honouring to him. Shared ministry experience contributes to the process of integration.

Relationship with Paul

The ninth context contributing to the process of integration is the relationship Timothy and Titus have with Paul.⁴⁷ Paul describes Timothy as "my true child in the faith" (ESV; γνησίῳ τέκνῳ ἐν πίστει, 1 Tim 1:2), which carries overtones of affection and intimacy, and is reinforced by a second use of "child" in 1 Timothy 1:18. In the syntax of the latter sentence, the inclusion of "Timothy, my child" emphasizes the importance of the relationship; if it had not been included the sentence would still have made grammatical sense. Paul's care for Timothy is that of a father for his own son. The basis for their relationship is their common faith in Christ, a faith which Timothy had proved to be real and genuine. As such, "my true child in the faith" also carries with it a sense of legitimacy, in contrast to the false teachers who do not stand in line with Paul's gospel.⁴⁸ Another indicator of the closeness of relationship is the closing of the letter in

---

45. Towner, *Letters to Timothy and Titus*, 457.
46. For discussion on how 2 Tim 1:6 relates to 1 Tim 4:14, see Towner, 457–60.
47. See also the earlier sections on *Example* and *Instruction* for material covering Paul's example and instruction.
48. Roloff, *Der erste Brief an Timotheus*, 15, 58; Mounce, *Pastoral Epistles*, 8.

which Paul directly addresses Timothy with "O Timothy" (6:20 ESV). After a string of imperatives, Paul finishes with a heartfelt plea for Timothy to guard the gospel and keep himself spiritually safe. Therefore 1:2 and 6:20 help to frame 1 Timothy as strongly relational. Integration for Timothy occurs within the context of his relationship with Paul.

Second Timothy reinforces and strengthens the picture of a deep bond between Paul and Timothy. This time Paul calls Timothy his "beloved child" (ἀγαπητῷ τέκνῳ, 2 Tim 1:2) whom he longs to see, and with whom he wants to experience the joy of being together (1:4). There is an emotional ache born out of an abiding love and concern for his co-worker. This is highlighted again in 2:1 as Paul addresses Timothy "You then, my son" (NIV; Σὺ οὖν, τέκνον μου), with "You" at the start of the sentence emphasizing the personal appeal.

In language almost identical to that of 1 Timothy 1:2, Paul describes Titus as his "true son in our common faith" (NIV; γνησίῳ τέκνῳ κατὰ κοινὴν πίστιν, Titus 1:4). Clearly Paul also shares a deep bond with, and affection for, Titus.

The depth of relationship contributes to integration in the lives of Timothy and Titus by reflecting the faith and love that are found in Christ (1 Tim 1:14). Just as Paul has experienced God's love, so he loves Timothy and Titus. The common faith and deep love they share is the basis for Paul's influence, so that when Paul gives them an instruction, they know it is motivated by his concern for them and others. As Smith points out, when Paul urged them to do something (e.g. 1 Tim 1:3; 2:1), "they were not commands for obedience, but persuasive appeals made within relationships of trust, established through, and shaped by, the gospel, and characterised by love and goodwill that sought the transformation of the addressees."[49]

Personal Responsibility

Personal responsibility is the tenth context contributing to the process of integration. Timothy is to take responsibility for his own growth. He is to give himself wholeheartedly to growing in ministry and godliness, paying attention to his own life and teaching (1 Tim 4:15–16). He is to train himself in godliness (1 Tim 4:7), cleansing himself so he is prepared for the good works God has for him (2 Tim 2:21). Timothy is to fan into flame his God-given

---

49. Smith, *Pauline Communities*, 288.

gift (2 Tim 1:6), join in suffering for the gospel (2 Tim 1:8), and be eager to present himself to God as a skilful handler of his word (2 Tim 2:15). He is also to take time to reflect on what Paul has written to him so that he can learn with God-given insight (2 Tim 2:7). The congregation provides a rich and diverse relational context in which to integrate theology, skills, and character, and Timothy needs to be a diligent and active participant taking responsibility for his own development. Similarly, Titus must exercise personal responsibility.

Training People to Train Others

The eleventh context contributing to the process of integration is training people to train others. Paul makes explicit in 2 Timothy 2:2 that Timothy is to train others to be integrated leaders. Training others in many ways brings together the contexts used to produce integration identified above. In the context of his own household and the congregation, Timothy must take responsibility for his own growth so that he can instruct others in faithful and contextually appropriate doctrine and behaviour. As he relates to those desiring to exercise leadership, he must pray for them, and model for them godly living, patient, gentle, and skilful instruction, a clear sense of identity, and willingness to suffer as he is engaged in gospel ministry.

In addition, Perry Stepp argues that the LTT would have been understood as "succession documents," meaning not apostolic succession but the protection and passing on of the gospel.[50] He especially sees this being focused in 1 Timothy, in which Paul has trained Timothy and entrusted him with the task of passing on the gospel tradition and authority to other leaders (1 Tim 5:22).[51] However, Stepp does not see the same emphasis on succession in 2 Timothy, and believes it is absent in Titus. Stepp's analysis that 2 Timothy does not fit with ancient parallels has rightly been critiqued by Jack Barentsen for not taking into account Timothy's task to train the next generation of leaders and its place in the purpose of the letter.[52] In addition, the previous chapter presented evidence of the skilful teaching of Titus that trained others, and this undermines Stepp's

---

50. Stepp, *Leadership Succession*, 1–14.
51. Stepp, 122–23, 130.
52. Barentsen, *Emerging Leadership*, 277–79.

claim that "Paul's instructions contain little information about the tasks a leader will perform or the abilities a leader needs to possess."[53]

There is an important connection between skilful teaching and the training of others.[54] The LTT emphasize sound teaching which not only enables the church to learn the truths of the faith, but also produces people who in turn can replicate godly belief and behaviour by teaching others. Teaching is not just the transfer of doctrine or helping others grow in godliness, though it certainly involves both; teaching is training people to teach and to train other people. The importance and skill of Timothy's training of others is reinforced by its multigenerational focus. Not only is he to train the next generation of overseers, deacons, and "faithful people"; he is training them so they have the integrated theology, skills, and character to train the subsequent generation. Similarly, as noted earlier, Titus not only appoints elders and trains various groups in the congregation, but he does it with such skill that they in turn can train others. The training of others acts as a method that reinforces the integration of theology, skills, and character in the lives of Timothy and Titus, as well as entrusting gospel leadership to others.

Summary and Implications

Having established that the content of integration in the LTT is theology, skills, character, identity, ministry, and suffering, in this chapter we have examined eleven contexts that contribute to the process of integration. The first eight contexts identified show that the LTT present a picture of integration happening in a richly relational context primarily centred on the church and including households and global mission. Within this domestic, ecclesial, and global matrix of relationships, integration is fostered through prayer, example, and shared ministry experience. The church also receives public and personal contextualized instruction through preaching, teaching, training, and the passing on of sound doctrine. Each of these contexts is also applicable to Timothy and Titus. In addition, three other contexts contribute to integration for Timothy and Titus. First, as part of God's people, Paul loves Timothy and

---

53. Stepp, *Leadership Succession*, 184.
54. Smith, *Pauline Communities*, 139–40, calls this "traditioning."

Titus deeply and they share a special bond as his children in the faith and co-workers. Second, they are to take responsibility for their own growth in godliness and ministry. Third, along with the overseers, deacons, and "faithful people," they are to train people who in turn will train others.

The process of integration in the LTT suggests three important implications. First, it demonstrates that integration will be taking place in churches as theology and character are brought together. Potential leaders who show signs of integration will emerge from within the church that has been cultivating the integration of belief and behaviour. Second, the findings suggest there is an appropriate place for further specialized training of leaders. Paul gave Timothy and Titus attention as he taught, nurtured, and trained them, and he expected them to respond by taking responsibility for their ongoing growth and development as gospel workers. Third, the first two implications suggest there is an interdependent relationship between them. Churches that foster integration will produce potential leaders who show by their lives that they are integrating theology and godly character. To do this, churches need healthy, integrated leaders who will promote integration within the congregation and so keep growing an environment that will produce potential, integrated leaders.

Discussion Questions

1. *How* does integration happen in your situation?

2. To what extent does theological education in your situation incorporate the various contexts outlined in this chapter?

3. If you could add one context listed in this chapter to what is currently happening in your situation, which one would you choose? Why? How would you go about adding it?

4. Do you agree with the statement that "there is an appropriate place for further specialized training of leaders"?

5. In your situation, what is the relationship between local churches and theological education institutions in fostering integration in emerging leaders?

Part C

Looking Forward

6

Integration in the Light of the Letters to Timothy and Titus

It is time to reintroduce theological education into the conversation; it has been calling for the integration of theology, skills, and character, and now there is the opportunity for it to hear what insights the LTT might have to offer. In this chapter we interact with current approaches to integration in theological education in the light of the findings on integration in the LTT.[1] As will be seen, there is much to be endorsed in current attempts in theological education to bring greater integration, but there are also some gaps. The chapter is organized according to what is being integrated and how this is being done. It turns out that there is already a great deal being attempted by the twelve approaches we heard from in chapter 2 which reflects the interests of the LTT.

The Content of Integration
Theology
We saw in chapters 3 and 4 that theology is one of the key pieces of content integrated in the LTT, and this is reflected in four ways in many of the proposals for integration in theological education: the content of theology, the experience of theology, the relationship of theology to practice, and the priority of theology.

---

1. As we noted in chapter 2, whether or not various voices in theological education identify the promotion of integration as their aim, they are nonetheless responding to the division of theory and practice. Implicitly or explicitly, they want greater integration.

First, there is much in common between the *content of theology* in some of the proposals for integration and the theology presented in the LTT. One approach treats missional theology as the focal point for the integration of theology, skills, and character, arguing that the *missio Dei* is the theological framework for the mission of the church.[2] This approach affirms God's plans centred on Christ for the redemption of the whole creation to his own glory, highlighting God's mission to the world through his church. This is in keeping with theology presented in the LTT, although there are differences between the individual letters. God's plans for the salvation of people stretch from one end of eternity to the other and are focused on the incarnation, death, and resurrection of Christ Jesus. As people who have experienced the transforming and renewing work of God's grace in Christ (Titus 3:3–8), the church holds up and holds out the mystery of godliness (1 Tim 3:14–16) as it speaks the truth and lives in a way that makes the teaching about God attractive to those around them (Titus 2:5–8). The LTT do not need to use "missional" as an adjective because the soteriological, christological, eschatological theology of the letters involves God's rescue mission for this world. Similarly, the LTT present the church as reflecting God's concern for the salvation of all people (e.g. 1 Tim 2:1–6). The missional theology central to some of the integration proposals is largely endorsed by the LTT.

Second, the *experience of theology* presented in many of the integration proposals is also endorsed by the LTT. The *theologia*, wisdom, worship, and personal and spiritual formation proposals strongly advocate that theological education should involve a personal knowledge of God. Theology is not only to be learned, but knowing God is to be experienced as a personal relationship. This corresponds to what is seen in the LTT. Paul overflows with praise for the grace and mercy he has experienced in Christ (1 Tim 1:12–17). Timothy has a sincere faith in Christ Jesus (2 Tim 1:5; 3:15), a faith Paul, Timothy, and Titus share in common (1 Tim 1:2; Titus 1:4); and all believers experience the washing of rebirth and renewal by the Holy Spirit through the saving grace

---

2. I recognize that missional theology is understood as a way of doing theology. Without at all neglecting this, scholars also treat missional theology as central to the content of theological education: i.e. the task of doing theology results in a truly missional theology. As such, missional theology can rightly be treated as part of the content of theological education. See, for example, Ott, *Beyond Fragmentation*, 205–11; Goheen, "Missional Reading," 308–14.

of Christ (Titus 3:4–7). The LTT present a picture of the knowledge of God being personal, experiential, and transformative, and so support the thrust of many integration proposals.

Third, the LTT help us understand the *relationship between theology and practice* in the integration proposals. The wisdom proposal argues that the knowledge of God is to shape a person's ways of acting. Similarly, missional theology treats theology as the driving force of good practice. The LTT support this view. The corporate worship of God's people is to be shaped by God's salvation priorities (1 Tim 2:1–7). God's people know how to behave based on the mystery of godliness (1 Tim 3:14–16) as the grace of God teaches them how to live (Titus 2:11–14). Paul and Timothy's conduct of ministry and willingness to suffer are driven by their understanding of the gospel of grace (2 Tim 1:8–14). Titus and Timothy are to teach the churches at Crete and Ephesus so they will know how to behave, for it is knowledge of the truth that leads to godliness (Titus 1:1). The examination of the wrong type of integration in the LTT has shown how unhealthy theology results in ungodly behaviour and practice. Across the LTT, the link is made that theology drives practice, whether good or bad.

Fourth, flowing on from the previous point, the LTT support the *priority of theology*, that is, theology being foundational, as expressed by some of the integration proposals. The review of current voices in chapter 2 demonstrated that theology was given priority in the missional theology proposal, in contrast to the *theologia*, reflective practice, and practical theology proposals which treat theology in a dialectical relationship with experience. In addition, while the curriculum proposal says the development of godly character and acquisition of skills are essential, biblical and theological knowledge is regarded as primary. Given that in the LTT theology is to drive practice, they support the view that theology should be regarded as foundational to the content of integration. This does not detract from the need for theological reflection based on experience; nor does it mean that the curriculum should be dominated by biblical and theological studies. Rather, it highlights that a biblical worldview will be grounded in God's revelation, and this is the starting point for integration. For example, in determining what is godly behaviour, an examination of the LTT shows that some personal behaviours are endorsed, and others are not. The assessment of those behaviours reflects the theological foundations, as theology is the lens through which behaviour and character are seen to be godly or ungodly. Similarly, theology is foundational in assessing whether the church should continue to proclaim Jesus Christ as Saviour when the surrounding culture claims there are many gods and other saviours. Reflecting on the prevailing culture is done through the lens of God's plans revealed in the gospel of Christ, resulting in the priority of mission for the church.

Many of the current voices in theological education argue for the importance of theology in the content of integration, and the LTT endorse this approach. There are strong parallels between the missional theology approach and the soteriological, christological, eschatological themes of the LTT; the knowledge of God is to be experiential, personal, and transformative; and the LTT see theology driving practice and so as foundational to the content of integration.

Character

The importance of godly character is a ubiquitous theme in the various proposals for integration. Although it is more prominent in some approaches (e.g. *theologia*, wisdom, worship, personal and spiritual formation, character education), all attempts to improve integration in theological education recognize the importance of producing graduates with godly character. The emphasis on godly character is also found in the LTT. Paul has been transformed from a blasphemer and persecutor of the church (1 Tim 1:13–14) to someone full of patience, love, and endurance (2 Tim 3:10). Timothy is to pay attention to his own life and set an example of godliness for the rest of the church (1 Tim 4:12–16). Potential elders and deacons are to be assessed for their godly character both in their own households and beyond the church (1 Tim 3:1–13; Titus 1:6–9), and the congregations at Ephesus and Crete are to be marked by love and good deeds towards one another and the surrounding society (1 Tim 1:5; Titus 2:1–10; 3:1–2, 12–14). The emphasis on godly character is also demonstrated by Paul's descriptions of ungodly behaviour, in which rejection of the truth produces corrupted minds and consciences, resulting in proud, arrogant, selfish behaviour (1 Tim 4:1–2; 2 Tim 3:1–5; Titus 1:10–16). The strong emphasis on godly character found across proposals for integration finds equally strong endorsement from the LTT.

Skills

We noted in chapter 1 that skills being part of integration is endorsed around the world. Yet despite this international consensus, the place of skills in proposals for integration is much less consistent than might be expected.

Chapter 2 demonstrated that *theologia* does not account for the place of skills in its scheme of integration. The worship proposal emphasizes the importance of practices but is limited in its scope, and personal and spiritual formation suggests practices that are not the most appropriate for developing skills. More positively, the wisdom proposal and that of reflective practice present themselves as inclusive of skills development, and the curriculum proposal also gives a place for skills in its effort to produce integration. The place of skills as part of integration is not consistent across the various proposals despite the internationally endorsed call for its inclusion.

Examining the LTT has shown that skills are included as part of the content of integration, but this is focused on Timothy and Titus and those they were to train for positions of leading and teaching in the congregation. Timothy is to be skilful in his teaching (2 Tim 2:24), and to train "faithful people" who will be competent to teach others (2 Tim 2:2). Overseers are to be competent stewards of God's people, able to teach and to lead and care for others (1 Tim 3:2–5; Titus 1:6–9). The LTT suggest that skills should be included as part of what is integrated in theological education, especially in terms of the development of leaders of congregations and other ministries.

This presents a challenge to some proposals in theological education. It is worth noting that *theologia*, worship, and personal and spiritual formation, which are perhaps the strongest advocates for the integration of godly character with theology, are also the weakest in their capacity to include skills as part of what is integrated. This is not to say that these proposals are philosophically opposed to the inclusion of skills, but it does suggest that the processes they use to bring about integration need to be supplemented with additional strategies.

Identity

The call for identity to be included as part of the content of integration varies, with some proposals more explicit than others. The *theologia*, wisdom, and worship proposals imply that identity would be part of integration through their focus on the personal knowledge of God being transformative for a student. In this sense they reflect John Calvin's claim that "man never achieves a clear knowledge of himself unless he has first looked upon God's face."[3] These proposals tend to focus on how knowing God transforms character, so the place of identity is more implicit. By contrast, the reflective practice and personal and spiritual formation proposals are much more explicit on the place of identity. Stache says theological education "is a process of moving deeper into who God is and who we are as God's creatures in God's world," and Naidoo says identity is important in formation because it provides a lens through which students appropriate knowledge, spirituality, and skills.[4] Peter Francis argues that reflective practice must include a focus on identity to deepen our understanding of who we are as God's children.[5] The curriculum proposal also includes identity as part of integration by virtue of its inclusion of personal and spiritual formation, and/or reflective practice.[6]

Identity is part of what is integrated in the LTT. All believers are the elect, belong to God and his household, and are heirs of eternal life (1 Tim 3:15; 2 Tim 2:10; Titus 1:1; 2:14; 3:7). Timothy is a "man of God" who teaches and leads with authority using the Scriptures (1 Tim 6:11; 2 Tim 3:17), and Paul includes his identity as an apostle and herald (e.g. 1 Tim 1:12–17; 2 Tim 1:8, 11; Titus 1:1).

This raises the question as to what extent the concept of identity expressed in the LTT is applicable for inclusion as part of integration in theological education. The identity of all believers as the elect people of God is certainly applicable today. Although Paul's identity as an apostle of Christ Jesus by the command and will of God is not transferrable, he does hold himself up as the model of a sinner on whom the Lord has had mercy as an example for others (1 Tim 1:16), making his identity as a sinner who has experienced mercy and grace applicable to all who believe. Timothy's identity as a "man of God" who teaches with authority using the Scriptures places him in line with a heritage of Old Testament prophetic figures, and yet he is not an apostle like Paul.

---

3. Calvin, *Institutes*, 1.1.2.
4. Stache, "Formation," 288; Naidoo, "Spiritual Formation," 188.
5. Francis, "Genuinely Reflective Ministry Practitioners," 197.
6. Shaw, *Transforming Theological Education*, 8–9; Goheen, "Missional Reading," 311, 329; Ott, *Beyond Fragmentation*, 233.

He stands as the link between the apostolic and post-apostolic eras and is expected to train up others so that he can pass on the mantle of authoritative teaching (2 Tim 2:2).[7] Those who follow Timothy as the authoritative teachers and trainers of the next generation could appropriately identify themselves as God's messengers.

In the light of this, the inclusion of identity as part of integration in theological education is justifiable according to the LTT. This applies not only to all believers in general, but also to those who lead and teach God's people.

Ministry

Ministry is heard as part of the content of integration from only some of the voices in theological education. Building on the work of Banks, Cronshaw places the practice of mission at the centre of his model of integrated theological education.[8] The practical theology and reflective practice proposals (almost by definition) begin with practice as the basis of theological reflection, and proposals such as those of Ott, Kreminski and Frost, Duraisingh, and Shaw bring ministry together with missional theology through the curriculum.[9] The *theologia*, worship, and personal and spiritual formation proposals do not seem to engage with ministry as part of their content, which echoes our previous observation about their lack of engagement with skills.

The LTT demonstrate that ministry is one part of what is integrated. Although ministry is hard work, it is motivated by hope in God the Saviour for the benefit of others (1 Tim 4:10), even when disciplining them (1 Tim 1:18–20). Timothy and Titus are to teach and lead for the benefit of those who listen, knowing they are accountable to God and the Lord Jesus. Likewise, the overseers, elders, and "faithful people" integrate theology, godly character, and skills with ministry. The church integrates theology and godly behaviour and it ministers both to believers (e.g. 1 Tim 5:1–6:2) and to society more broadly (e.g. Titus 3:1–2, 14). Thus, the inclusion of ministry in the content of

---

7. Griffiths, *Preaching in the New Testament*, 53–54.
8. Cronshaw, "Reenvisioning Theological Education," 13.
9. Ott, *Understanding and Developing*, 276–77; Kreminski and Frost, "Missional Leadership," 180–83; Duraisingh, "Ministerial Formation," 41; Shaw, *Transforming Theological Education*, 101.

integration in the models of Banks and Cronshaw, as well as the curriculum proposal involving mission and reflective practice, finds support from the LTT.

Suffering

A particular contribution of 2 Timothy to our discussion is its emphasis on suffering as it is integrated with theology, godly character, and ministry. All who are faithful to the content of the gospel and its proclamation will be opposed, including Paul, Timothy, Titus, and those in leadership positions, such as overseers. Endurance is theologically motivated, knowing that those who do endure will reign with Christ Jesus (2 Tim 2:12), as they endure by God's power (2 Tim 1:8). More broadly, all believers will be persecuted for seeking to live a godly life (2 Tim 3:12). This requires faithful perseverance (2 Tim 2:10–13), understanding that the eschatological judge will reward all who maintain faith (2 Tim 4:8).

This contribution from 2 Timothy highlights a gap in the proposals for integration in theological education. Across the wide spectrum of proposals, the issue of suffering is not included as part of the content of integration.[10]

Summary

There is therefore much in common between the LTT and the voices in theological education outlined in chapter 2 regarding the content of integration. The investigation in chapters 3 and 4 demonstrated that theology, skills, character, identity, ministry, and suffering constitute the content that is integrated in the LTT. Putting suffering to one side for the moment, the rest all find places in the various proposals for integration, with the most common feature being godly character, which was included across all proposals. Perhaps this can be regarded as a universal reaction against a theological education that is purely cognitive, and a recognition of the many demands of ministry. The content that is being integrated in theological education resonates with, and is endorsed by, the LTT.

However, what the different proposals are seeking to integrate is not uniform. There is a clear trend with the *theologia*, worship, and personal and

---

10. Salier, "Facilitating Student Formation," 324. Salier makes the point from Rom 5 that suffering has a place in the character formation of students.

spiritual formation proposals not giving attention to skills and ministry but instead focusing on character and, more implicitly, identity. A less noticeable trend is the lack of focus on identity and the personal experience of theology in the missional theology proposal. It is ironic that proposals for integration focused on character and identity neglect skills and ministry, and those focused on theology neglect identity and relational knowledge of God! While all the content identified by the LTT, except for suffering, is included across the breadth of proposals for integration, only the curriculum proposal includes most of the content of integration.[11]

Given that the content of integration identified in the LTT finds expression in various integration proposals, even if inconsistently, it raises the question as to whether "integration" should be redefined. It has been widely accepted that integration involves theology, skills, and character, yet the content of the proposals keeps moving beyond this trio, even though what is added varies. In practice, the content of integration is recognized as broader than theology, skills, and character, a situation endorsed by the LTT.

The Process of Integration

Integration in the LTT occurred in a richly relational context primarily centred on the church and also including domestic households and global mission. The church received public and personal contextualized instruction, and prayer, example, and shared ministry experience also contributed to the process of integration. Paul's deep bond with Timothy and Titus, their personal responsibility for growth in godliness and ministry, and the training of people who would train others, are three additional factors that contributed to the process of integration for Timothy and Titus. This section assesses the *processes* offered in various integration proposals against those identified in the LTT, and finds that what is currently being attempted in theological education has much in common with those in the LTT.

---

11. Ott, *Understanding and Developing*, 303–38; Shaw, *Transforming Theological Education*, 4–9; Goheen, "Missional Reading," 327; Kreminski and Frost, "Missional Leadership," 176–79.

Proposals Focused on Christian Paideia

Chapter 2 showed that the *theologia*, wisdom, worship, personal and spiritual formation, and character education approaches emphasize the process of *paideia*, even though some use the term and others do not. Farley says his *theologia* proposal is an attempt to "reconceive theological education as a *paideia* and not merely a scholarly learning or learning for practice."[12] The wisdom proposal regards the process of *paideia* as a key to the formation of wise people.[13] In the worship proposal, people are enculturated to think, act, and love in a certain way in the context of, and for the benefit of, the church and wider society, suggesting this proposal engages in *paideia* even if it does not use the term. And as an example of the personal and spiritual formation proposal, Aaron Ghiloni says that personal formation involves "nurture, direction, discipline, socialization, and inculturation," which approximates *paideia*.[14] These proposals emphasize the importance of personal and affective processes for the learning and formation of students. They do not reject biblical and theological instruction, but do not want theological education to be limited to this. The worship and personal and spiritual formation proposals also incorporate church as a context for learning. In addition, the curriculum proposal, when it incorporates personal and spiritual formation, also includes *paideia* among the processes used to shape students.[15]

Collectively, the proposals that give a prominent place to *paideia* incorporate many of the practices that promote integration identified in the LTT. These practices are personal and relational, include church as a learning context, and promote prayer, while not marginalizing the place of instruction.

Proposals Involving Relationship, Example, and Shared Ministry Experience

A prominent trio of interrelated factors contributing to the process of integration identified in the LTT are relationship with Paul, example, and shared ministry experience. Paul loves Timothy and Titus, sets them an example, and shared

---

12. Farley, *Theologia*, 194.
13. Hodgson, *God's Wisdom*, 111–24; Treier, *Virtue*, 30; Vanhoozer, "From Bible to Theology," 243.
14. Ghiloni, "Is Formation Education?," 30.
15. Shaw, *Transforming Theological Education*, 101; Goheen, "Missional Reading," 311, 329.

life and ministry with them. In turn, Timothy and Titus are to do the same in the congregation as they train others.

This trio of practices is also found in Banks's Jerusalem paradigm, an example of a place association model. Based on the practice of Paul and his band of co-workers, Banks argues that learning the Bible and theology should involve all of life's relationships, and therefore theological education should be partially or completely field based as the student and teacher engage in ministry together in a communal setting.[16] Similarly, Allan Harkness argues for ministry training to occur in the context of doing ministry as the teacher acts as a mentor for the student, thus making the relationship between them crucially important.[17] It is also common for various curriculum proposals to involve field education, in which a student learns under the supervision of an experienced practitioner.

Relationship, example, and shared ministry experience are not only for the field but also for the classroom. Shaw says "the quality of the relationship which exists between instructor and students is one of the foremost characteristics of excellence in teaching" and is built through trust as teachers establish "a form of in-class hospitality."[18] Banks echoes this, saying that "others learn best when we share *ourselves* as well as our *knowledge* with our students."[19] The classroom becomes the context of shared experience. Beyond the classroom many theological education institutions include some form of mentoring between students and faculty. Shaw says "this intimate and personalized approach to learning can be among the most significant and life-changing educational experiences a student has while engaged in theological studies."[20]

The reflective practice proposal also draws on the experience of students in ministry to promote integration. However, while it has the capacity to include relationship and example between teacher and student, the focus is on the experience of the student.

---

16. Banks, *Reenvisioning*, 126, 143, 157.
17. Harkness, "De-Schooling the Theological Seminary," 150–51.
18. Shaw, *Transforming Theological Education*, 262.
19. Banks, "Paul as Theological Educator," 52.
20. Shaw, *Transforming Theological Education*, 112.

Therefore, across the various proposals, including curriculum and reflective practice, we find personal relationship, example, and shared ministry experience being deployed as practices to promote integration, and this reflects approaches also found in the LTT.

Proposals Involving Contextualization

Contextualization was one of the practices Paul used to integrate theology and practice, and this is found in a number of proposals promoting integration in theological education. The practical theology and reflective practice proposals call students to engage with their context through critical reflection, resulting in a theology grounded in their context and practice. Missional theology takes a similar approach. Ma sees theology arising out of the church in mission – that is, theology is developed in a context, and this in turn drives contextualized theological education.[21] This approach is reflected in Cronshaw's model which includes local and multicultural contextualization, and also finds concrete expression in examples of curriculum proposals, such as those of Shaw and Goheen.[22] These proposals are built on missional theology and want to produce graduates who can contextualize their theology and ministry. This reflects Paul's approach to contextualizing theology and practice found in the LTT.

Training People to Train Others

One of the practices that contributes to the process of integration in the LTT is the training of people who in turn train others. Just as Paul had trained, and continued to train, Timothy and Titus, so they were to train and appoint overseers, deacons, and "faithful people." These church leaders were in turn to train the next generation of leadership.

The discussion surrounding integration in theological education is evidence of the sector's desire for the highest-quality training experience for students, which is exhibited in the breadth of proposals. The adult teaching and learning approach is a prime example of the efforts to enhance the learning experience of students. However, when compared with the LTT, the various

---

21. Ma, "'Life' in Theological Education."
22. Cronshaw, "Reenvisioning Theological Education," 13; Shaw, *Transforming Theological Education*, 21–24; Goheen, "Missional Reading," 313, 327–28.

voices in theological education do not focus on equipping students with what is necessary to train others.[23] Students are learning, but are not being shown how to pass on this learning to those they will serve in ministry contexts in such a way that it will in turn be reproducible. The LTT highlight an important gap in the current proposals in theological education to produce integration.

Revisiting Paideia *in Theological Education*

Our interaction with the various proposals that promote integration in theological education points to them incorporating many of the practices identified in the LTT. One of the most prominent of these is *paideia*, which is particularly seen in the *theologia*, wisdom, worship, personal and spiritual formation, character education, and curriculum proposals. However, I suggest that the understanding of *paideia* being used in discussions of theological education needs reworking in terms of both its content and its process.

Kelsey understands *paideia* to be "a process of 'culturing' the soul, schooling as 'character formation.'"[24] As we have seen earlier, this emphasis on the enculturing of a person in order to form him or her is woven through a wide range of proposals. However, this understanding of *paideia* as character formation neglects to include skills, contrary to the shape of *paideia* in the Graeco-Roman world. Plato recognized rhetoric as a skill, and Aristotle argued that young people should be taught only those skills that helped them grow in virtue.[25] For Cicero, a skilled orator who is virtuous is both rare and embodies all that is honourable, while Quintilian's ideal leader will be a person of good character, wide knowledge, and skilful rhetoric.[26] *Paideia* in the Graeco-Roman world was not focused only on forming character; it also involved skills as it prepared people to be citizens. Paul has retained the components of *paideia* involving theology, skills, and character, and filled it with fresh Christian content.

---

23. Noelliste identifies that theological educators need to be trainers of the trainers but does not provide a model of how this might happen. Noelliste, "Handmaiden," 28.
24. Kelsey, *Between Athens and Berlin*, 6; Edgar, "Theology of Theological Education," 210.
25. Plato, *Gorg.* 456d–457c; Aristotle, *Pol.* 8.1337b.
26. Cicero, *De or.* 2.85; Quintilian, *Inst.* 12.1.25.

If Kelsey has underemphasized the skills content of *paideia*, the work of Banks highlights that the process of *paideia* may also have been misunderstood. Banks claims that the division between theory and practice cannot be fixed by "*paideia* revolving around *theologia*," and therefore he advocates for learning to take place through hands-on partnership in mission, in keeping with the pattern he discerns between Paul and his co-workers.[27] However, *paideia* in the Graeco-Roman world involved experience. Aristotle said experience was important for growing the knowledge of universal principles into practical knowledge applicable to real-life circumstances.[28] Xenophon said experience in the training of young men produced high-quality thinking, speaking, and action.[29] An elite Roman young man attached himself to a rhetorician, gaining an intimate understanding of the model's way of living. Experience brought together knowledge, skill, and character as part of the process of *paideia*, and this is evident in the LTT through modelling, and as Paul, Timothy, Titus, overseers, "faithful people," and the church share in ministry together. In addition, the relationship between Paul and Timothy and Titus also contributes to the process of integration. By bringing attention to experiential learning, Banks helpfully turns the spotlight on an aspect of *paideia* that was not featured in Kelsey's proposal. But in advocating for ministry experience in addition to *paideia* and *theologia*, Banks does not recognize that in the Graeco-Roman world, the process of *paideia* already involved hands-on, experiential learning, in relationship with a more senior model or mentor.

These observations have implications for Kelsey's Athens–Berlin typology of theological education, and the subsequent place association models built upon it. Kelsey critiques what has been inherited from Berlin for its focus on the professional training of clergy for the task of church leadership; theology has been reduced to understanding the skills and tasks needed for the clerical role and is in tension with growing in the knowledge and love of God.[30] Given, though, that the development of skills was part of *paideia*, growing in skills and growing in character were not thought of as being in tension with each other

---

27. Banks, *Reenvisioning*, 142–46.
28. Aristotle, *Metaph.* 1.981a.
29. Xenophon, *Cyn.* 1.18.
30. Kelsey, *Between Athens and Berlin*, 12–18; Farley, *Theologia*, 84–88, 130.

in the Graeco-Roman world. Moreover, the LTT demonstrate that theology, skills, and character are integrated. The tension Kelsey perceives between the *paideia* of Athens and the professional training of Berlin is at least partly a result of not including skills in the understanding of *paideia*.

Where Kelsey is right is to critique Berlin for its elevation of *Wissenschaft* – research built on critical presuppositions and techniques. The theology of the LTT is built on the epistemological claim of God's revelation and stands in contrast to the emphasis placed on reason in the Graeco-Roman world. By elevating reason above revelation, *Wissenschaft* has in a sense "returned to Athens." Banks's Jerusalem model is a response, at least in part, to what he perceives to be a weakness in Kelsey's proposal. As has been argued above, Banks's assessment is built on the assumption that Athens (i.e. *paideia*) did not involve experiential learning.

This critique of Kelsey and Banks raises the question of whether a more comprehensive understanding of the content and process of *paideia* would have produced different models from those constructed around the Athens–Berlin typology.

Cronshaw's model (see fig. 6.1) identifies some of the features of integration in the LTT. Geneva points to God's revelation of himself (theology); Athens points to transformed character in response to God; Berlin points to the inclusion of skills for ministry; Jerusalem points to the experience of ministry and mission; Auburn and New Delhi point to engaging the world in a contextualized manner.

By comparison, the integration presented in the LTT is summarized in figure 6.2. In contrast to Cronshaw's model, theology is foundational to the content of integration in the LTT (left-hand column), and the practices give more emphasis to relational aspects of the process of integration (right-hand column). In addition, there is no place for suffering or the training of people in the existing approaches. The inner arrows indicate the content and process that apply to the whole church. The outer arrows indicate that, as well as the same content and process relevant for the church also applying to Timothy and Titus, there is the additional content of skills, and three additional factors of relationship with Paul, personal responsibility, and training people to train others.

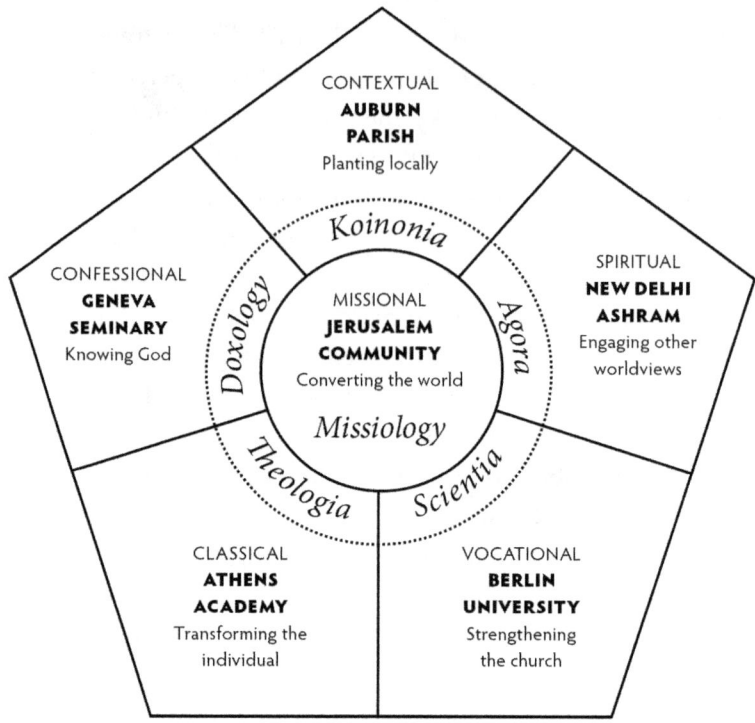

Figure 6.1 Cronshaw's Model[31]

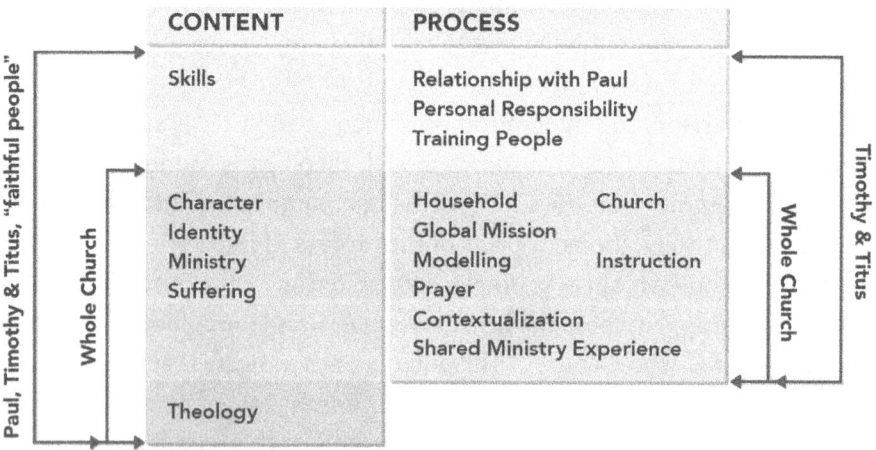

Figure 6.2 Integration in the LTT

---

31. Adapted from Darren Cronshaw, "Reenvisioning Theological Education and Missional Spirituality," *Journal of Adult Theological Education* 9, no. 1 (2012): 13.

Summary

The content, and the factors contributing to the process, of integration in the LTT find widespread but inconsistent expression in the current proposals of theological education as they promote integration. This is encouraging, for not only does it suggest theological education is heading in a healthy direction, but the endorsement of the LTT adds greater strength to its theological moorings. Nevertheless, the inconsistencies and gaps suggest there is still room for further work to bring greater cohesion to the good work going on to cultivate integration.

Discussion Questions

1. What is theological education doing well? Spend some time thanking God for this.

2. This chapter highlights that, when compared with the LTT, some approaches of theological education do not give attention to skills and ministry, and others neglect identity. If you were to assess your own context in the light of the LTT, what conclusions would you come to?

3. Suffering is not found in any of the current approaches of theological education. Why?

4. If there was one change you could make to promote integration, what would it be?

7

Eight Principles for Integration in Theological Education

Why do we do what we do in theological education? Why have seminaries and Bible colleges at all? After all, they require resources such as buildings, libraries, books, journals, computers, e-resources, as well as people such as administrators and students and faculty. To be good stewards of all that God has given us will require a clear sense of purpose surrounding all that we are doing. Taking this a step further, *how* do we determine the "what" and "why" and "how" we are to be doing in theological education? On what grounds do we make these decisions? And how might our conversation between theological education and the LTT help us?

Ball identifies that theological education has at least four philosophical rationales: the historical or traditional, theological, ecclesiological, and the pedagogical.[1] He says the historical or traditional rationale justifies theological education according to what has always been done.[2] According to the theological rationale, the purpose of theological education is to grow people in the knowledge of God; the ecclesiological rationale says theological education is to serve the mission of the church; and the pedagogical rationale shapes theological education according to how teaching and learning are to occur.[3] Ball's categories will be adapted, so this chapter is organized around

---

1. Ball, "Where Are We Going?," 11–12.
2. Ball, 11.
3. Ball, 12.

the theological, ecclesiological, and pedagogical rationales. Interaction with the historical rationale is beyond the scope of this chapter.[4] Based on the conversation between theological education and the LTT, we offer eight principles for integration.[5]

The Theological Rationale of Theological Education

The first principle is that theology, as the knowledge of God and his plan of salvation in Christ, is foundational to theological education. The first finding to emerge from the survey of theological education in chapter 2 was that most theological educators see integration flowing from a presupposition of personal, relational faith. The call for integration in theological education reflects the dissatisfaction over the split between theory and practice, a split that has been expressed, in part, in the claim that dry, rational, critical study has usurped the relational and experiential knowledge of God.[6] A consistent theme across many of the proposals is that, not only must theology be part of integration, but theology must also involve knowing God personally in addition to knowing about God.[7]

Knowledge of God and relating to him is a combination endorsed by the LTT. First, the LTT affirm that God can be known through the knowledge of the truth (1 Tim 2:3; 2 Tim 1:10; Titus 1:1). Second, not only can God be known, he makes himself known through his Scriptures (2 Tim 3:16) and Jesus Christ (1 Tim 1:13–15; 3:16; 2 Tim 1:10; Titus 2:11–14). Third, the LTT present God's revealed plan of salvation for humanity. This plan is focused on Christ's death and resurrection (1 Tim 1:15; 2:3–5; 3:16; 2 Tim 1:8–10; 2:8–11; Titus 3:3–7) and stretches from before time (2 Tim 1:9; Titus 1:2) to the return of Christ (1 Tim 6:14; 2 Tim 4:1; Titus 2:13). The missional theology model aligns with this plan of salvation.

---

4. For historical surveys, see Farley, *Theologia*; Ott, *Understanding and Developing*, 15–86.
5. There are parallels between Ball's categories and Ott's scheme of integration on the existential, functional, material, and structural levels. See Ott, *Beyond Fragmentation*, 238–41.
6. Cannell, *Theological Education Matters*, 101–2; Farley, *Theologia*, 10–11.
7. Cannell, 91–94; Charry, "Educating for Wisdom," 296; Edgar, "Theology of Theological Education," 213.

Fourth, the LTT present knowing God as experiential and profoundly transformative; through God's mercy and grace expressed in Christ, people are released from slavery to worldly passions and are cleansed and renewed (Titus 3:3–7), and this experience of knowing God integrates with personal identity. Combined with the personal knowledge of God in the LTT is the "knowledge of the truth" (Titus 1:1). Timothy and Titus are to teach so that the believers will know what is true about God and his purposes. Likewise, the elders, deacons, and "faithful people" are to hold to the truth and teach it to others, part of which is to warn against those who do not hold to the truth. Knowing God experientially and knowing the truth are held together in the LTT.

We have also seen that in the LTT, theology is foundational to godly character and sound ministry practice. The mission and behaviour of the church reflect God's christological, eschatological plan of salvation, and the church is to be led by those who hold to the truth, exhibit godliness, and lead and teach skilfully, knowing they are accountable to God.

In addition, through their use of *paideia* vocabulary, the LTT present God correcting and instructing people to turn away from ungodliness and the devil in order to live godly lives full of good deeds by means of the knowledge of the truth found in the gospel (2 Tim 2:25; Titus 2:15) presented by Timothy and Titus. God is the ultimate educator who works through his servants to transform people.

In the light of the foundational place the LTT give to theology as the knowledge of God and his plans in its full experiential and cognitive sense, its centrality to theological education is not axiomatic, it is essential.[8] Nor can it be assumed, given the warnings the LTT provide about the destructive effects of false teaching.

> ### Principle 1:
> Theology, as the knowledge of God and his plan of salvation in Christ, is foundational to theological education.

---

8. Dockery, "Theological Education," 17; Jaison, *Towards Vital Wholeness*, 76–78; Harkness, "Introduction," 12.

The Ecclesiological Rationale of Theological Education

The second principle is that the church has theological priority and responsibility for theological education. The LTT present the church as a key part of God's purposes in this world. The church is God's household, "the pillar and bulwark of the truth," heirs of eternal life, and his agents in the here and now (1 Tim 3:15; Titus 2:10; 3:7). As such, the ontology of the church is theologically grounded. Based on this, theological education institutions are to serve the church.[9] The church is established by God as part of his plans in this world, but theological education institutions cannot claim this for themselves. Similarly, mission agencies, parachurch organizations, and specialist ministries may bring focus and expertise to their area of mission and ministry, but their ontology is not theologically grounded. They are not an end in themselves but serve the mission of God's church.[10] The same can be stated about theological education institutions.[11] The theological mandate of the church establishes the church's responsibility for theological education.

> **Principle 2:**
> The church has theological priority and responsibility for theological education.

The third principle is that the goal of theological education is to equip those who will equip the church as the people of God. One of the themes consistently found in what is written about theological education is a call for it to be refocused for the benefit of all believers, rather than for the benefit of clergy and vocational ministry workers. Farley critiques theology for being reduced to the theory about the tasks clergy are required to perform, resulting in a failure to educate laypeople.[12] In a similar vein, Alan Roxburgh says that "overcoming the professional, clergy-shaped leadership models is an essential

---

9. Akin, "Theology for Church," 389–90; Jaison, 25–27.
10. Newton, *Mentoring Church*, 115–30.
11. Shaw, *Transforming Theological Education*, 60.
12. Farley, *Theologia*, 129–31; Kelsey, *Between Athens and Berlin*, 223.

shift toward a missional leadership."[13] Duraisingh says "the primary concern for us cannot be ministerial education as such, but rather the equipping of people in local congregations for mission."[14]

Our examination of the LTT found a two-tiered approach to integration.[15] At the congregational level, theology and godly character are to be integrated with identity, ministry, and suffering for living the Christian life. For Timothy and Titus, and those who lead the church, the extra dimension of skills is added. It is the role of Timothy and Titus to teach, model, and train the next generation of leadership within the congregation so that they will be equipped to teach and care for the church. The development of integrated believers in the congregation comes through the ministry of integrated leaders. The approach presented by the LTT reflects Ephesians 4:11–16 in which the evangelists, pastors, and teachers equip the saints for ministry so that the body of Christ grows in maturity.[16]

In the light of the LTT, integration should be developed in both vocational ministers and laity, recognizing that integration for vocational ministers will include an extra dimension of skill development, and the primary developers of integration among the laity are to be the vocational ministers. Putting these two together, it is not unreasonable to say that one of the skills that needs to be developed in vocational ministers is the skill to train, grow, and equip other people. This is in keeping with the practices of teaching, instruction, and training identified in the LTT; teaching and training people involves equipping them to replicate what they have learned by teaching and training others. In other words, theological education equips those who will equip the church. Darrell Guder states it like this:

> The proper outcome of missional theological education, built and shaped by a missional hermeneutic, is that the community of equipped witnesses in a particular context will live out their

---

13. Roxburgh, "Missional Leadership," 200.
14. Duraisingh, "Ministerial Formation," 35.
15. Noelliste, "Handmaiden," 18–19, 28. Noelliste uses a three-level approach to describe theological education. Level 1 is the training of trainers, level 2 the training of clergy, and level 3 the clergy training the laity.
16. Dockery, "Theological Education," 18.

> lives intentionally as Christ's witnesses wherever and however God sends them. What that community of sent ones should experience when gathered is continuing formation and equipping, centred in the biblical word interpreted missionally. This needs to become the priority of the missional community, the community seeking to respond to that mandate, and therefore it must become the priority of our theological education: the biblical equipping of equippers of the saints.[17]

The need for integrated leaders who can equip laypeople for mission in the world has been brought into sharp relief in the last forty years as the collapse of Christendom has been increasingly recognized. The missional church movement and missional theology have called for the church to recapture its identity as God's agent in reaching a lost world.[18] The LTT present the church as the primary place where God's people will be equipped for mission. A missional church will also be a church being trained for mission by its pastors, teachers, and evangelists.[19] As such, the LTT envision that the training of pastors, teachers, and evangelists will involve training them to train others.

An objection that could be raised to this paradigm is that currently not all students in theological education are wanting to be trained for vocational ministry. Oxenham says that "students have changed, and many now come to theological training as adults, either looking to enhance their lay vocations or simply desiring personal development."[20] In surveying the history of theological education in Australia, Ball notes the same shift from the 1970s, when most students entered theological education institutions to prepare for vocational ministry, to the current goal of personal development.[21] "The attitude of a tertiary student has thus permeated the broader theological sector. The wider social, educational and aspirational profile of students has developed

---

17. Guder, "Missional Hermeneutic," 289–90; Noelliste, "Handmaiden," 18–19.
18. E.g. de Gruchy, "Theological Education"; Goheen, "Missional Reading," 302–7; Guder, "*Missio Dei*," 65–68.
19. Guder, "Missional Theology," 49; Kreminski and Frost, "Missional Leadership," 176–79.
20. Oxenham, *Character and Virtue*, 12.
21. Ball, "Thematic History," 91.

a consumer approach."²² He backs this up by pointing out that about half of graduates do not end up serving in vocational ministry.²³ In the light of this, Ball and Oxenham echo the calls of Duraisingh and Roxburgh when they urge theological education to do more to equip laypeople so they are able to engage with the contemporary society they are a part of.²⁴

The call to equip the laity is entirely consistent with the LTT and the rest of the New Testament. However, the shift in the goals of students from vocational ministry preparation to personal development can be understood as indicative of a failure of church leadership to equip the laity. Laypeople have been turning to theological education institutions looking for the tools of understanding they have not been given in their local congregations. In response, theological education institutions have adapted to cater for this demand. But this does not address the root cause of the problem. Without a deeply integrated theological education designed to produce vocational ministry workers who can equip members of local congregations to engage in God's mission in the world, the church will continue to offer inadequate training. Rather than theological education institutions becoming increasingly focused on equipping laypeople, the LTT point out that we need integrated leaders who can lead and equip the people of God to grow as integrated congregations that can engage in God's mission of salvation. This is expressed by Mark Bailey when he says, "It is the role of the seminary to equip and encourage transformed students to serve in transformed churches that will transform the world for the name and fame of Jesus Christ."²⁵

> **Principle 3:**
> The goal of theological education is to equip those who will equip the church as the people of God.

---

22. Ball, 91.
23. Ball, *Transforming Theology*, 54.
24. Ball, "Where Are We Going?," 16; Oxenham, *Character and Virtue*, 17–19.
25. Bailey, "Foundation and Shape," 32.

The Pedagogical Rationale of Theological Education

The fourth principle is that in theological education, experience has sequential priority in learning, and theology is authoritative. The survey in chapter 2 identified that theological education is making increasing use of adult teaching and learning theories and reflective practice. These include a focus on student-centred learning, acknowledging that students bring with them a range of experiences from outside theological education which influence and shape their learning, and a recognition that the general pattern of learning begins with the learner's experience. In this sense, experience has a sequential priority in the learning process. Reflecting upon the experience can be done theologically, personally, and practically in order to produce a holistic concept of what has been learned.[26] Active experimentation and further concrete experience provide the opportunity to test new theories and provide for further learning.

The development of this "new knowledge" betrays the tension between the need both to contextualize theology and to maintain and pass on the inherited theological tradition. The LTT affirm both contextualization (see below) and "holding to the truth." Within the learning process, something will prove to be authoritative in shaping the learning derived from the interaction of experience and theorization, and the argument of the LTT is that that authority rests with theology as the knowledge of God. At this point, theology has priority because it demonstrates that God has revealed himself and his understanding of the world in which we live; theology becomes the authoritative lens through which to view the world. Reason, experience, and tradition are also resources that inform this reflective process, but theology is primary.[27]

> **Principle 4:**
> In theological education, experience has sequential priority in learning, and theology is authoritative.

How do the content and process of integration relate to one another? Theological education recognizes that learning involves what is to be learned,

---

26. Francis, "Genuinely Reflective Ministry Practitioners," 192.
27. Francis, 194–95.

how it is to be learned, and where it is to be learned.[28] The relationship between the content and how it is integrated will be looked at first, before turning to examine where integration happens.

The fifth principle is that theological education requires a congruence between what is being integrated and the practices used. Shaw points to the need for the practices being used to promote integration to match the content of what is being integrated.[29] An example he cites is the powerful effect that apprentice-style learning can have on promoting growth in godly character and identity.[30] And the opposite is true as well: a practice ill-suited to and ill-matched with its content undermines the integration process.

The LTT highlight a suite of factors that combine to produce integration. The range of factors provides the flexibility needed to match the content being integrated, and these factors are more adaptable and comprehensive in their ability to facilitate integration than some of the current proposals in theological education.

> **Principle 5:**
> Theological education requires a congruence between what is being integrated and the practices used.

The sixth principle is that theological education requires a variety of learning contexts, providing both involvement and distance, and in which there is congruence between what is being learned and the learning context. Harkness makes the point that the setting in which learning takes place needs to align with the learning objectives.[31] In applying this principle he says,

> When seminaries have as their major aim the comprehensive know-do-be formation of people for Christian ministry, such

---

28. Shaw, *Transforming Theological Education*, 40–44; Ott, *Understanding and Developing*, 274–80; Oxenham, *Character and Virtue*, 261–350.
29. Shaw, 41–42; Oxenham, 318.
30. Shaw, 73.
31. Harkness, "De-Schooling the Theological Seminary," 146; Brynjolfson, "Missionary Training and Spirituality," 199.

> formation will take place most effectively in settings which provide for similar aspects to be expressed, and a significant proportion of this necessarily will need to be in the setting of a non-schooling paradigm.[32]

Facilitating integration does not equal uniformity of educational setting. An example of the application of this principle is seen in the strength of Banks's Jerusalem model in which he insists that learning *about* mission and ministry happens most effectively in the context of being involved *in* mission and ministry.[33] Another example is the growth in character and identity that occurs through personal mentoring.

A second educational principle that informs this discussion is that of "involvement and distancing." Ott makes the case that involvement in ministry is needed, rather than just talking about it, and distance from ministry is needed in order to reflect upon it.[34] In addition, reflection needs to include others experiencing similar involvement in ministry, such as a peer group or cohort of students. Stereotypically, theological education has been strong on the distance part of the equation and weak on involvement. This has created a mismatch between the learning objectives and the learning context, particularly in the areas of character formation and skills development.

The LTT demonstrate that integration takes place in a relationally rich matrix involving household, church community, the personal example of key figures, and the shared experience of life and ministry. There are also opportunities for instruction, and the contextualization of theology and practice. In addition, there is the ministry of training others. This suggests that the primary learning context for the formation of character and ministry skills will be the church because it provides a context that aligns with the learning objectives and personal participation.[35] Rather than only being a context in which learning from the theological education institution is applied, church is a learning context in its own right.

---

32. Harkness, 146; Collinson, "Making Disciples," 17.
33. Banks, *Reenvisioning*, 142.
34. Ott, *Beyond Fragmentation*, 231–32.
35. Ott, *Understanding and Developing*, 213–18, 265–68.

It is also worth recognizing that mission agencies, parachurch organizations, and specialist ministries may also provide appropriate contexts for learning. As they serve the overall mission of the church, they can also provide relationally rich contexts for the learning of character and ministry skills in keeping with what is seen in the LTT.

While church provides some instruction, theological education institutions provide a context for greater depth of instruction, as well as the opportunity for students to appropriately distance themselves from the activity of ministry for reflection, and to reflect and learn with others undergoing the same ministry training.

> **Principle 6:**
> Theological education requires a variety of learning contexts, providing both involvement and distance, and in which there is congruence between what is being learned and the learning context.

The seventh principle is that theological education involves strong personal relationships between faculty and students. In presenting his Jerusalem model, Banks argues that the relationship between Paul and his band of ministers is that of co-workers or colleagues rather than master and apprentices.[36] He describes the relationship between Paul and Timothy as "more akin to the affectionate bond that can exist between a father and his adult son than between a superior and a subordinate."[37] In addition, Banks argues that in regard to personal example, "in the main, we should regard imitation of Paul as more a general theme in Paul's teaching about the Christian life and only a secondary feature in his teaching about the conduct of ministry," although he does concede this is more prominent in the LTT given that they are written to individuals.[38]

Banks is right that the LTT portray deep and affectionate relationships between Paul and Timothy and Titus. Such affection, though, does not run

---

36. Banks, *Reenvisioning*, 116.
37. Banks, 119.
38. Banks, 121.

counter to Paul's ongoing training of Timothy and Titus as he continues to instruct them through his letters. They have shared, and continue to share, in ministry together, and part of Paul's ongoing training of them involves reminding them of the Lord's grace and mercy in Paul's conversion, Paul's own life and teaching, and his suffering for the gospel. While Banks is right that there is deep relationship and shared ministry between Paul and Timothy and Titus, in that context, Paul continues to train them by instruction and example. They are not just work colleagues but brothers in Christ serving in ministry together, and Timothy and Titus do not share the same seniority as Paul; he is an apostle and they are being trained by him.

Ball makes the observation that, as a result of the increasingly higher qualifications in Australia over the last thirty years, a shift has occurred in the way those who teach in theological education regard themselves; the pastor-teacher has been replaced by the teacher-researcher.[39] A possible danger this could suggest is that teachers have become more relationally distant from those they teach, and in the way they teach, which is antithetical to the picture the LTT present of Paul's training of Timothy and Titus. Perhaps the faculty of theological education institutions should carry the title of "ministry trainers" or "ministry equippers."[40] To be a "trainer" or an "equipper" shifts the emphasis from content to relationship: a lecturer gives a lecture (content) but a trainer trains people to train others. This would broaden the sense of what faculty do; they continue to lecture and teach, but lecturing and teaching are only part of relating to students as they equip and train them for ministry.

> **Principle 7:**
> Theological education involves strong personal relationships between faculty and students.

The eighth and final principle is that theological education requires collaborative partnerships between the church and theological education institutions involving faculty and students. In his book on Bonhoeffer's work

---

39. Ball, "Thematic History," 93.
40. I am grateful for this thought from Tim Patrick in conversation with Peter Adam.

in seminaries, Paul House argues for a theological education built around a highly relational, seminary-based approach to Christian community.[41] Shaw, while endorsing the importance of strong relationships between students and mature leaders, notes the difficulties of turning the ideal into a reality, including the recruiting and training of mentors, unsuitable matches between students and mentors, an unwillingness of institutions to give credit in the curriculum for what is done in mentoring, and a lack of willingness from students to admit to weaknesses, especially in honour–shame cultures.[42]

Cahalan also sees the need for strong personal relationships between students and trainers, and advocates for the involvement of ministry-active church leaders. She says, "Mentors – people whom they both observe and are observed by in practice – provide the best learning situation for the advanced beginner. Expert pastors and ministers are excellent mentors if they can explain their thinking behind a practice and guide and critique the student in their performance and skill development."[43] Although this does not solve Shaw's point about the difficulty of recruiting and training mentors (it would still need to happen), it reflects the call for much stronger partnerships between the church and theological education institutions.[44]

The examination of the LTT made clear that the church was the chief relational and ministry context in which Timothy and Titus were operating as Paul continued to train them. A further point can be made. We have also seen that Timothy and Titus were training and equipping the next generation of leaders in the congregations. Timothy and Titus were not the pastors of the congregations at Ephesus and Crete; they were appointing and training elders and overseers for those roles. Yet Timothy and Titus clearly had a role in teaching and modelling the Christian faith as they trained others. In a sense, they were acting as "theological educators" embedded in the lives of the congregations.[45] While the LTT endorse current calls for a relationally rich environment in theological education, they also raise the possibility

---

41. House, *Bonhoeffer's Seminary Vision*.
42. Shaw, *Transforming Theological Education*, 113.
43. Cahalan, "Integration," 392.
44. Ott, *Understanding and Developing*, 270–71; Banks, *Reenvisioning*, 156; Harkness, "De-Schooling the Theological Seminary," 152; Akin, "Theology for Church," 394.
45. Banks, *Reenvisioning*, 257.

that the lecturers and teachers should go to the students in the context of the congregation, rather than, or in addition to, asking the students to come and join in the community life of a theological education institution. Such an approach could strengthen the partnerships between the church and their training organizations. It might also help address the difficulty of finding appropriate mentors because lecturers would be working alongside their students in ministry and providing them with feedback. Lecturers would also work alongside current ministry practitioners, coaching them in the mentoring of students, and thus broadening the pool of skilled mentors.

> **Principle 8:**
> Theological education requires collaborative partnerships between the church and theological education institutions involving faculty and students.

Summary

Based on the conversation between theological education and the LTT, we have presented eight principles for integration organized under the categories of the theological, ecclesiological, and pedagogical rationales for theological education:

1. Theology, as the knowledge of God and his plan of salvation in Christ, is foundational to theological education.
2. The church has theological priority and responsibility for theological education.
3. The goal of theological education is to equip those who will equip the church as the people of God.
4. In theological education, experience has sequential priority in learning, and theology is authoritative.
5. Theological education requires a congruence between what is being integrated and the practices used.
6. Theological education requires a variety of learning contexts, providing both involvement and distance, and in which there is congruence between what is being learned and the learning context.

Eight Principles for Integration in Theological Education

7. Theological education involves strong personal relationships between faculty and students; and
8. Theological education requires collaborative partnerships between the church and theological education institutions involving faculty and students.

A recurring theme that emerges from the discussion above is the importance of community. Students require strong communities involving their peer group, faculty, and other believers from both their local congregation and their theological education institution. Within the contexts of these communities, students can sit under God's word together, pray together, serve together, love and encourage one another, as well as be corrected, rebuked, and equipped for every good work in life and ministry. This is in keeping with the pattern of a relationally rich learning environment we have seen in the LTT.

Discussion Questions

1. What functions as the rationale(s) for theological education in your context?

2. What are the strengths of theological education in your situation according to the principles outlined in this chapter?

3. Principle 3 says "the goal of theological education is to equip those who will equip the church as the people of God." Do you agree? Why or why not?

4. This chapter outlines eight principles for theological education. Are there other principles you would add to the list that are relevant to your context and can also be supported by the LTT?

8

A Possible Way Ahead

This chapter offers a fresh proposal to enhance integration in theological education. After recapping some of the key existing proposals, the discussion attempts to build on their good work by combining the principles identified in chapter 7 and Christian *paideia* into a concrete proposal that includes a curriculum.[1]

I am not suggesting this is the only way to conduct theological education. Context is vital; what is appropriate in one context might not be in another. The goal of this chapter is to show that all we have covered so far is not just theoretical but can be turned into practice. Hopefully this will further stimulate your thinking and encourage you in your own context.

Current Proposals

The current proposals of Goheen, Shaw, Ott, Oxenham, and Haar capture most closely the principles articulated in the previous chapter. The new proposal builds on their strengths, and so some brief additional comments are required to fill out what we have already seen so far.

Goheen offers the model shown in figure 8.1.[2] He describes the training as done in a "missional key."[3] Goheen's model reflects some of the key principles identified earlier:

---

1. The curriculum involves all that happens as part of the learning, including the syllabus, beyond-classroom activities, and the culture of the theological education institution. See Jaison, *Towards Vital Wholeness*, 35–37.
2. Goheen, "Missional Reading," 311.
3. Missional Training Center, "Theological Education."

1. It places the knowledge of God in the gospel at the centre (Principle 1).

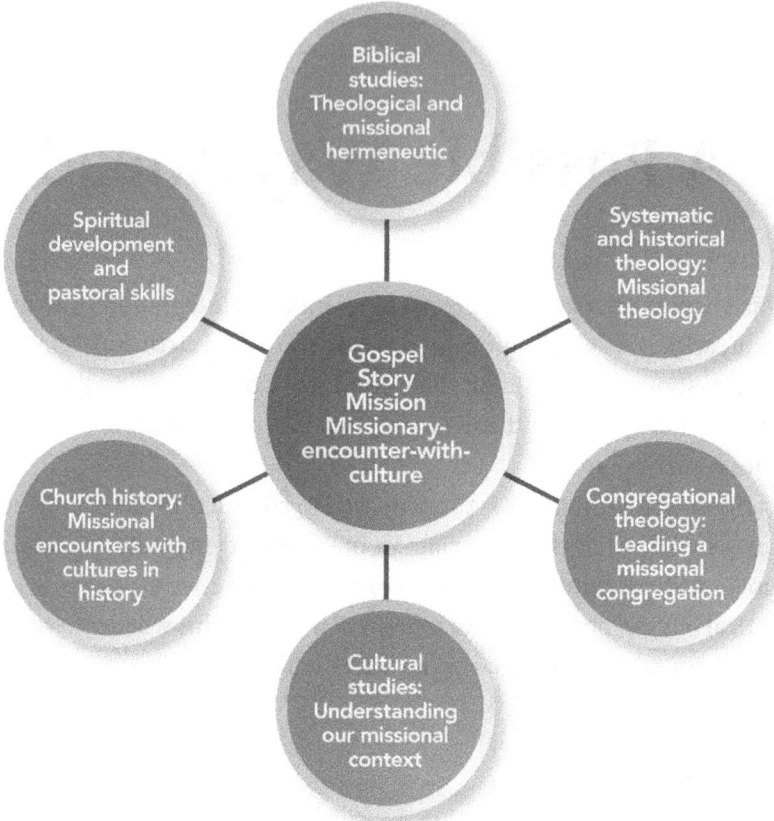

Figure 8.1

2. It aims to equip pastors to equip others (Principle 3), though Goheen's model also includes training those whose ministry is public life rather than vocational ministry.[4]
3. It seeks to build strong relationships within a cohort of twelve to sixteen students who are together for four years (Principle 7).[5]

---

4. Goheen, "Missional Reading," 309–10.
5. Missional Training Center.

4. The course is designed to connect with the local church, allowing the mentoring of church leadership to develop skills, character, and devotional life (Principle 8).[6]
5. The place of cultural exegesis is in harmony with the use of contextualization.
6. Assignments are designed to connect academic learning with the congregation. Students also continue working full-time in their current ministry setting because the course runs at half-time pace with classes at 6 a.m. – 9 a.m. or 6 p.m. – 9 p.m. This suggests a variety of learning contexts through collaboration between churches and the seminary (Principles 6, 7, and 8).[7]

Two difficulties are apparent with Goheen's model. First, it is an MA course and therefore available only to graduates.[8] Second, the combination of full-time work and part-time study raises the concern as to whether the involvement–distance spectrum is weighted too heavily towards involvement and does not provide adequate space to reflect upon ministry and do the required assignments.

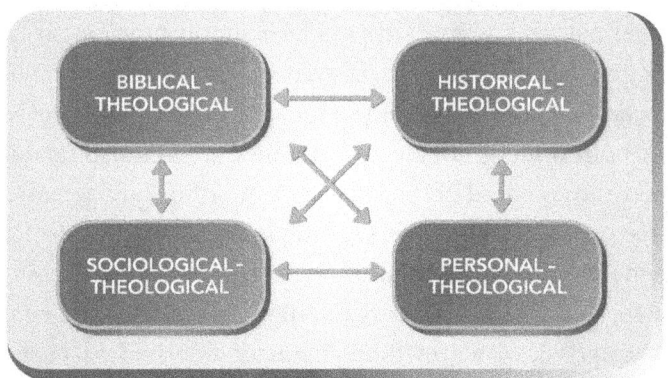

Figure 8.2

---

6. Missional Training Center, "Theological Education."
7. Missional Training Center, "Cohorts."
8. A similar comment can be made about Kreminski and Frost's Master of Missional Leadership.

Shaw presents the model of Arab Baptist Theological Seminary (ABTS) as four curricular lenses, as shown in figure 8.2.[9] Material reflecting each of the lenses is integrated as part of a five-week module.

Although the diagram expresses that there is no "centre" to the curriculum, clearly it has a strong engagement with biblical-theological material, thus reflecting Principle 1. The ABTS curriculum also gives credit for learning activities that happen beyond the classroom, including church ministry and theological reflection on life and ministry, thus exhibiting collaboration between church and theological education institution (Principle 8), and the need for a variety of learning contexts and processes that match what is being learned (Principles 5 and 6).[10] Students are required to meet with a mentor no less than seven times during the year, suggesting a strong personal relationship between students and those helping train them (Principle 7).

Ott cites the model of the Reformed Church of Switzerland, shown in figure 8.3.[11] A strength of this proposal is the organized and structured collaboration between the university and church, reflecting Principle 8. There is also a range of learning processes and contexts involved (Principles 5 and 6). There is a clear goal to equip students so they can in turn equip the church as the missional people of God (Principle 3).

One potential weakness of Ott's model is simply how long it could take to complete. Students are required to spend six years of preparation before being certified as competent, which could be too long for students. The requirement to complete both undergraduate and graduate studies also raises a question as to whether the standard of the bachelor's program carries sufficient depth. Despite these concerns, the model Ott cites is a clear attempt to bring together the complementary learning environments of university and church.

Character education is the organizing principle for the curriculum in Oxenham's proposal, with growth in character a desired goal across all units or courses and expressed in classroom learning and assessment tasks, reflecting Principles 5 and 6 to some degree. There is a development across the three-year

---

9. Shaw, *Transforming Theological Education*, 3.
10. Shaw, 6.
11. Ott, *Understanding and Developing*, 341.

program, beginning with more content and finishing with increased practical activity.[12]

UNIVERSITY COMPONENT	CHURCH COMPONENT
BACHELOR'S PROGRAM *6 semesters* Students acquire knowledge in all areas of basic theology through lectures, seminars, and writing papers and other assignments.	**MENTORING** Beginning with the first semester, students are mentored by trained individuals by the church.
	ECCLESIOLOGICAL-PRACTICAL SEMINAR A five month internship outside the university setting combined with group supervision
MASTER'S PROGRAM *4 semesters* Students expand their knowledge and are able to present an overview of the central themes in the field and to articulate the state of current theological debate.	**DEVELOPMENTAL APTITUDE ASSESSMENTS** Four evaluations interspersed throughout the entire four semesters
	STUDY INTERNSHIP A year-long training experience in a church, with supervision by specially trained pastor. Includes twelve different week-long courses.
	CERTIFICATE OF COMPETENCY Examination at the end of the course of study to determine skills acquired during training, using a recognized competency grid.
	CONTINUING EDUCATION IN THE FIRST YEARS OF PASTORAL MINISTRY

Figure 8.3

Oxenham identifies five models regarding the venue of theological education: online learning; a retreat centre in which students learn in intensive mode; an embedded city model focused on learning through weekend and night classes; a local community model with students meeting in churches two or three times a week; and a full-time residential campus model.[13] He favours the last option, with its strong sense of community providing the environment

---

12. Oxenham, *Character and Virtue*, 324.
13. Oxenham, 311–16.

for character development through a combination of modelling from the faculty, habituation, and service, and so reflecting Principle 8.[14]

Oxenham's model presents a clear attempt to integrate the knowledge students are learning with their growth in character in every aspect of their course. There is also an emphasis on the strong personal relationship between the students and faculty, and the community as a whole.

Haar's proposal is for a distributed model of theological education.[15] He distinguishes this from distance education or online learning by calling for a combination of face-to-face classroom learning, spiritual formation under the guidance of a mentor, experiential learning, online participation and video, and contextual-based learning.[16] The aim is to draw together the college, church, and student's context as places of learning.[17] The strength of this proposal is its recognition that a combination of contexts are needed for effective learning and therefore the deliberate establishment of partnerships between churches and theological education institutions, so reflecting Principles 5, 6, and 8. However, the proposal in its current form is short on specifics regarding how it would function in practice.

One final observation that can be made of the current models is the general absence of discussion regarding the contribution of households to the training of students, which stands in contrast to what we have identified in the LTT. Three suggestions might provide clues as to why this is the case. First, it may be that the contribution of the household is subsumed under the category of character within theological education. The character of students is considered important and is demonstrated within their households, but the household is not treated as a separate category, meaning it does not achieve prominence in discussion of the various models. Second, Western individualism can lead to underemphasizing the valuable contribution a student's web of relationships – including his or her household – plays in the student's formation. Third, a diminished sense of collaboration between churches and theological education institutions may have resulted in undervaluing the importance of

---

14. Oxenham, 338–45.
15. Haar, "Re-Imagining Theological Education"; "Distributed Model."
16. Haar, "Distributed Model," 7.
17. Haar, "Re-Imagining," 56; "Distributed Model," 7.

the household. The theological education institution may not ever meet the student's household simply because there is no working relationship with the local church. Principle 6 helps address this issue.

Details of a Fresh Proposal

Our proposal builds on the strengths of Goheen, Shaw, Ott, Oxenham, and Haar, and incorporates the eight principles identified earlier with Christian *paideia*. An additional element that is drawn upon is the Ministry Training Strategy (MTS).[18] In Australia, MTS offers a two-year apprenticeship scheme for people prior to formal theological study. An apprentice serves in ministry alongside an experienced ministry practitioner (or practitioners) and is given informal feedback as well as formal reviews. Schemes using an apprentice model like MTS exist around the world.[19] The strength of MTS has been that, when done well, students begin theological study already well equipped in ministry skills, have experienced the excitement and disappointments of ministry, and often have a list of experience-prompted questions they want to investigate. However, unwittingly MTS has perpetuated the division of theory and practice as two years of high-level ministry involvement is followed by three or four years of extensive study.

Theological education that enhances integration needs to be intentionally designed by aligning curriculum, teaching and learning methodologies, and assessment with the desired goal of the entire process.[20] The aligned process is represented in figure 8.4.[21]

---

18. Ministry Training Strategy, https://www.mts.com.au.
19. E.g. St. Mary's Cathedral (Synod of the Diocese of West Malaysia), www.stmaryscathedral.org.my/ministries/mit/; Capitol Hill Baptist Church, Washington, D.C., www.capitolhillbaptist.org/pastoral-internship; St. Helen's Bishopsgate, London, www.st-helens.org.uk/about/associate-scheme.
20. Hockridge, "Rethinking Our Approach," 201–2.
21. Shaw, *Transforming Theological Education*, 52–53; Jaison, *Towards Vital Wholeness*, 124–26; Cunningham, "Assessment beyond the 4bs," 33–34.

Figure 8.4

Building on Jaison's definitions, I understand these terms in the following way:[22]

- Inputs are the resources allocated (both planned and in reality) to the task of theological education.
- Outputs are the activities of a theological education institution and the resulting imprint on the students.
- Outcomes tell us how graduates live and minister beyond their theological education.
- Impact speaks of the ongoing, long-term influence of graduates on their context.

The impact of theological education has recently been framed in terms of the effect of the church on society.[23] This has been critiqued by Oxenham for running the risk of being mechanistic and utilitarian – in other words, if the curriculum is right it will produce societal change, and the value of theological education is that it functions to facilitate that change.[24] He calls for a more deontological approach in which there is intrinsic value in knowing God for its own sake.[25] He says that "to *see* God ranks higher than to *serve* God."[26] However, to polarize knowing God and the impact of theological education is unhelpful. Growing in the knowledge and love of God is vital, and it should result in fruitful living for God (John 15:1–8; Col 1:9–14).

An important contribution of the aligned process outlined above is that it allows theological educators to plan with the desired goals in mind. By "reverse engineering" the process, each aspect can be aligned. What then do the LTT tell us about each part of this process?

---

22. Jaison, *Towards Vital Wholeness*, 124–25.
23. Shaw, *Transforming Theological Education*, 52–53; Das, "Relevance and Faithfulness," 24–26.
24. Oxenham, "Impact Agenda," 120–23.
25. Oxenham, 124–25.
26. Oxenham, 125.

Our examination of the LTT highlights the desired *impact* of God's church in his world. In 1 Timothy, Paul encourages Timothy to teach the church so they will live in keeping with their identity as the household of God in the face of false teaching (1 Tim 3:14–15). As the pillar and bulwark of the truth, they are to hold to the truth of God's word, and hold out that truth in word and deed because it is God's desire to save people (1 Tim 2:1–4; 5:1–6:2). In 2 Timothy, the church is called to persevere in faith (2 Tim 2:11–13), despite godly living bringing persecution (2 Tim 3:12), knowing they will be rewarded when Jesus returns (2 Tim 4:8). Titus is to appoint elders and teach so that the church will be fruitful and productive in their good deeds and therefore effective in their witness (Titus 2:10; 3:14). According to the LTT, the desired impact of God's church in the world is to bear witness to the truth so that people may be saved, and to nourish them in that truth so they may persevere in faith, living fruitful and productive lives of good deeds, until the return of Christ.

To achieve what has just been described requires certain *outcomes* of theological education. Each of the LTT points to the importance of the truth of God's word being taught for the health of the church, especially in the face of false teaching. To be healthy in their life together as God's people and in their external witness, the church requires sound doctrine. The sound doctrine of the gospel is to be guarded and passed on. Transformation of the church occurs through the current generation of leadership teaching the truth and passing it on by entrusting it to new leaders.

To ensure this outcome will require certain *outputs* from theological education. If we draw on the principles developed above, Principle 3 states that "the goal of theological education is to equip those who will equip the church as the people of God." This output goes beyond current approaches to integration in theological education which aim to transform students through the integration of theology, skills, and character. Our proposal builds on this by taking it a step further. The conversation between the LTT and theological education has shown that churches require integrated leaders who have the capacity and ability to train and equip the next generation of integrated leaders, who in turn will do the same. The outcome of theological education must not simply be students who are transformed through integration; the outcome should be "reproducible transformation."[27] Graduates who integrate theology, skills, and character should be able to train and equip the people of God so that they integrate theology and character to act as God's witnesses to the world. In addition, integrated graduates should be able to grow other integrated leaders. "Reproducible transformation" through integrated graduates is an outcome in keeping with the desired impact of theological education.

To summarize so far, the framework of input, output, outcome, and impact can be given some detail in the light of the LTT (see fig. 8.5).

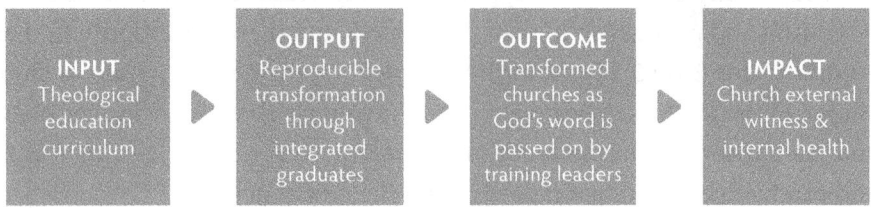

Figure 8.5

The *input* of a theological education institution is expressed in its curriculum. In what follows, just one curriculum is proposed as an example of how the principles might be embodied, and which serves the desired output, outcome, and impact.

It is recognized that the contexts in which theological education is conducted vary greatly, so any proposal must be held loosely.[28] While what follows is simply one expression of a curriculum rather than a definitive model, nonetheless its value is in demonstrating that the principles developed in chapter 7 can be fashioned into an on-the-ground, working curriculum. Two versions are offered: the first for online distance education, and the second for face-to-face education.

---

27. This is different from Brock who says learning that reproduces maintains a group or society, as against learning that equips people with the skills to bring about transformation. See Brock, "Integrated Curriculum Design," 286–87.
28. Thompson and MacLeod, "To the Ends of the Earth," 113–25.

Online Theological Distance Education

Online Theological Distance Education (OTDE) is defined as a mode of theological education in which there is no requirement for students to meet face to face with faculty or other students.[29] To begin our discussion of OTDE, we must first look at the rationale for using it as a mode of education. We propose that Principles 2 and 3 developed earlier provide an appropriate foundation for the use of OTDE and advance the current debate on the issue.

A major study in 2017 reported that a significant motivation for theological education institutions offering OTDE was to attract new students and therefore be more financially efficient.[30] Similarly, Christopher Jackson notes it is primarily external pressures such as student numbers and finances that are driving the adoption of OTDE by theological education institutions.[31] In response to such pragmatic concerns, scholars have sought to provide biblical and theological justification for OTDE as a legitimate mode for the training of students. Annang Asumang says that the LTT provide a biblical mandate for OTDE, arguing that, even though he was absent, Paul continued his formation of Timothy and Titus through the exhortations and directives contained in his letters; in a similar vein, theological education institutions are able to effectively train students even though there is no face-to-face contact.[32] It is therefore legitimate for theological education institutions to embrace the use of OTDE, providing it fits with the mission and values of the institution.[33]

Our argument is that the principles outlined in chapter 7 provide a more appropriate foundation for the use of OTDE. Principle 2 outlines that the church has priority and responsibility for theological education, and therefore theological education is to serve the interests of the church. This runs counter to the pragmatic motivations for using OTDE in the interests of the survival

---

29. Nichols, "Akadameia as Paradigm," 7.
30. Miller and Sharen, *(Not) Being There*, 22–23.
31. Jackson, "Social Presence," 4–5.
32. Asumang, "Spiritual Formation at a Distance," 23–30. For more detailed discussion of the place of the Pauline epistles in the formation of congregations and the implications for OTDE, see Jones et al., *Teaching the World*, 31–47; Forrest and Lamport, "Modelling Spiritual Formation from a Distance," 110–24.
33. Jones et al., 154–55; Stache and Nessan, "Digital Teaching," 35.

of any given theological institution; rather, the use of OTDE must serve the interests of the church.

Principle 3 says that the goal of theological education is to equip those who will equip the church. This extends and deepens the current discussion in two ways. First, rather than anchoring the rationale for using OTDE in the mission and values of an institution, its use is tied to the overarching goal of theological education, thus transcending the differences that may exist between institutions. Second, Principle 3 provides a biblical understanding for the goal of theological education under which the biblical grounds for making use of the mode of OTDE may sit. The current debate seeks to biblically legitimize OTDE as a *mode* of education; Principle 3 provides the ecclesiological rationale and framework for making use of that mode.

Having looked at the rationale for using OTDE, we turn now to the curriculum, which is outlined in figure 8.6.

YEAR 1	YEAR 2	YEAR 3	YEAR 4
TE Institution	**TE Institution**	**TE Institution**	**TE Institution**
4 Foundational online units	6 Integrated learning units	6 Integrated learning units	4 Integrated learning units
Church			**Church**
Ministry involvement and training, and training others (e.g. evangelism, leadership, pastoral care, contextualization) under direction of ministry trainers	**Church** Ministry involvement and training, and training others, under direction of ministry trainers	**Church** Ministry involvement and training, and training others, under direction of ministry trainers	As per years 1-3 and includes requirement of more in-depth training of lay people

Figure 8.6

The curriculum reflects Principle 6, which calls for a variety of learning contexts involving distance for reflection and involvement, and congruence between what is being learned and the learning context, through a combination of contexts provided by the church and the theological education institution.

As part of this, students learn through a variety of activities and assessments so that there is congruence between what is being integrated and the practices used, as stated in Principle 5. In addition, students draw on their experience of ministry as part of their learning, reflecting Principle 4.

To structure the curriculum in such a way requires collaborative partnerships between churches and theological education institutions, thus reflecting Principle 8. The collaborative partnerships can be seen to be mutually beneficial. First, theological education institutions offering OTDE make it possible for students to stay and learn within their home ministry contexts, and not have to uproot themselves and their families, thus making theological education more accessible for a greater range of people. Indeed, this is seen as one of the chief benefits of OTDE.[34]

Second, by learning within their home ministry contexts, students are provided with congruence of learning, practice, and context, outlined in Principles 5 and 6.[35] As they participate in ministry, students are provided with training, mentoring, and feedback.[36] Making use of the home ministry context reflects what Stephen Lowe and Mary Lowe call an "ecosystems" approach to learning which takes holistic account of the variety of contexts in which students learn, recognizing that no one context can match all the learning needs of a student.[37] Indeed, Mark Nichols views the church as such an important learning context that he believes OTDE is not able to offer effective integrated training of students without it.[38] This pushes our proposal from a strictly online model to a hybrid or distributed model. Thus, the provision of online classes makes theological education more accessible for the church, and the involvement of the church as a learning context makes OTDE more effective in training students; collaborative partnerships between theological education institutions and churches are mutually beneficial.

---

34. Jones et al., 154, 162; Roberts, "Online Learning."
35. Hockridge, "Challenges for Educators," 157; Sharen and Campbell-Reid, *Learning Pastoral Imagination*, 18.
36. Naidoo, "Ministerial Formation."
37. Lowe and Lowe, "Ecosystems Model," 97; Naidoo, "Formational Learning."
38. Nichols, "Akadameia as Paradigm," 14–15. Nichols's research argues that students involved in their local churches experience a fuller and more rounded formation. See Nichols, "Comparison of the Spiritual Participation"; "Formational Experiences."

First-year students are introduced to biblical units in Old Testament, New Testament, and Bible overview, thus reflecting that theology is foundational, as outlined by Principle 1. In the following years, units integrate the various disciplines of theological education (e.g. OT, NT, Theology, Ministry, Ethics) with practical and reflective components which develop skills, character, and the training of others. Not only does this reflect Principles 3, 5, and 6, it also points to the importance of the intentional design of learning units to enhance the learning experience for students.[39]

Current best practice suggests that each course should begin with a period of intensive time together (e.g. a weekend or a block of classes) to allow faculty and students to forge strong bonds which serve as the "relational capital" upon which online classes are built, and this reflects Principle 7.[40] This proposal involves the faculty teaching online classes and sharing in the mentoring of students in collaboration with their church-based mentors, thus furthering the depth of the relationships between students and faculty.[41]

Face-to-Face Theological Education

The learning context in the first year of the program is weighted to involvement in church ministry. Students serve as apprentices in ministry alongside a church staff member and a lecturer, who jointly share in training and mentoring them, reflecting the collaborative partnership between church and theological education institution outlined in Principle 8. Students are equipped in ministry skills such as preaching, pastoral care, evangelism, contextualization, and leadership as they are given opportunities to participate in ministry. In this way, right from the start of the course, students are beginning to train and equip other people, in keeping with Principle 3. They are led by their mentors through theological, personal, and practical reflection upon their ministry experience. They are also mentored in identity and personal and spiritual formation as they participate with their ministry trainers in prayer and other spiritual disciplines and share in the joys and sufferings of ministry. Students receive

---

39. Hockridge, "Reimagining Christian Formation"; Asumang, "Spiritual Formation at a Distance," 13.
40. Miller and Sharen, *(Not) Being There*, 42; Naidoo, "Ministerial Formation," 5.
41. In "Formational Learning," 6, Naidoo says the quality of formation depends on faculty involvement.

formal and informal feedback from their trainers regarding their character. The involvement in ministry, and reflection upon ministry with strong supervision and mentoring, embodies Principles 4, 5, 6, and 7 with experiential learning in a variety of learning contexts, congruence between what is being learned and the context used, and strong personal relationships between faculty and students. The ministry experience with its skills and character development is formally recognized as part of the degree award and is woven throughout the four-year program.

YEAR 1	YEAR 2	YEAR 3	YEAR 4
TE Institution	**TE Institution**	**TE Institution**	**TE Institution**
4 Foundational face-to-face units	6 Integrated learning units	6 Integrated learning units	4 Integrated learning units
Church			**Church**
Ministry involvement and training, and training others (e.g. evangelism, leadership, pastoral care, contextualization) under direction of ministry trainers	**Church** Ministry involvement and training, and training others, under direction of ministry trainers	**Church** Ministry involvement and training, and training others, under direction of ministry trainers	As per years 1-3 and includes requirement of more in-depth training of lay people

Figure 8.7

In addition, first-year students take four foundational face-to-face units across the year, providing the platform for further study in the coming years. Two of the units are paradigmatic in nature, focusing on how the story of the Bible is a coherent whole and understanding what the gospel is, while the other two units are introductory surveys of the Old and New Testaments. Together they reflect Principle 1, that theology is foundational. Some of the assignments require application to the ministry context, such as writing a set of Bible studies or running a training seminar at church introducing a book of the Old Testament that has been studied. Trainers also begin to draw upon the students' growing knowledge as they reflect biblically on their experience of ministry, thus reflecting Principle 4.

At the end of the first year, following a formal review involving the student and the ministry trainers, there is the option to exit the course. It may be that together the student and trainers conclude that it is unwise for the student to continue; or perhaps the student is unsuitable; or the most appropriate way for the student to serve God is as an active lay member of his or her congregation and so the student will return to the workforce. If students exit at this point, they have had a year of ministry experience, personal mentoring in identity, character and skills development, and foundational biblical training, and this is something to be celebrated. In most accreditation systems this would equate to being awarded a diploma or graduate diploma.

In the second and third years of the program, the balance between church and classroom is more evenly weighted, providing a variety of learning contexts in keeping with Principles 5 and 6.[42] Continuation in ministry provides the opportunity for reflective practice, as ministry experiences raise theological issues, and the growing body of biblical and theological knowledge is drawn upon for reflection upon practice. The ongoing mentoring from the students' ministry trainers continues, and bonds of trust and affection grow as they share life and ministry together (Principle 7).

Original languages can be learned in the second year and applied later in the course. The face-to-face units studied in the second, third, and fourth years are integrated in their content and delivery. For example, a unit on "Creation" might be introduced by the Ministry lecturer and two of the students who outline the real-life situation of a mother of two who is struggling with transgenderism. Together the class come up with a list of issues they see as relevant to the situation. In the next part of the unit, the Old Testament lecturer leads the class through a detailed exegesis of Genesis 1–3. Building on this, the Theology lecturer leads the class in synthesizing other parts of the Bible and theological thought as they develop a doctrine of creation. In the last section of the course the Ethics lecturer, with the Ministry lecturer, leads the class in discussing the topic of "identity and sexuality" in the light of their exegetical

---

42. For an argument for the benefits of student involvement in ministry while studying, see Rogers and Winstead, "Pedagogical Lessons."

and theological understanding of creation by focusing on the case study of the lady struggling with transgenderism.

Units such as this integrate theory and practice as they begin with a real-life experience and are reflected upon biblically, theologically, ethically, pastorally, and practically, and so express Principle 4. The use of team teaching also models the integration of different theological disciplines, both in content and in delivery. Such units also prepare students to engage with contemporary issues, enabling them to equip others. Although the balance of the content will vary from unit to unit, the basic structure and philosophy applies to each one.

In the final year of the program, the weighting shifts again more heavily in favour of ministry participation as the students prepare to make the transition from student/apprentice to vocational ministry worker. Although students will have been equipping others through their ministry involvement during the course (e.g. leading a Bible study group with a trainee co-leader), preparation for this transition part of their ministry involvement in their final year requires students to be involved in training members of the congregation at greater depth, thus reflecting Principles 2 and 3. This is done in concert with, and under the supervision of, their ministry trainer. For example, a student might run a three-week course on "Christians and the Media." The student will be responsible for organizing and promoting the course. He or she might involve a journalist the first week, a film-maker the second week, and a musician the third week, and also personally give some biblical input aimed at training laypeople to engage with the issues in a prayerful, well-informed, and biblically shaped way.

The curriculum would require a range of approaches to assessment, reflecting Principles 5 and 6. Integrated theological education must be holistic and include assessment of a student's behaviour, affections, character, and skills, as well as cognitive understanding.[43] For example, the proposal provides the opportunity to assess cognitive understanding through a formal written paper, and at the same time incorporate feedback from a ministry trainer about the student's skills in preaching, a reflective exercise about a pastoral conversation, or an interview about the student's growth in godliness. There is also the opportunity to incorporate in the assessment a focus on training

---

43. Shaw, *Transforming Theological Education*, 201–15.

others in what the student is currently learning. For example, a written essay can include a section asking the student to explain how he or she might teach the key points of an essay to his or her Bible study group in an engaging and appropriate manner. In reflecting Principle 3, the assessment tasks can be used to reinforce "reproducible transformation."[44]

As part of the proposal, faculty are involved with the students in ministry in a local church setting and mentoring is shared with church staff, capturing Principles 7 and 8. In this way, the lecturer who might teach biblical studies in the classroom is serving with students in a church setting as they engage in evangelism together. Just as the students come from local churches to the theological education institution, faculty go from the institution to the churches.

The involvement of faculty as outlined above requires a paradigm shift in the understanding of their role and focus. First, faculty shift from being scholars and researchers to trainers of trainers. Research and scholarship become servants to inform the training of students as trainers of others. Second, there is a shift from "learning and teaching" to "learning for teaching." In recent years the application of adult learning principles to theological education has shifted the focus of teaching from being teacher-centred to student-centred learning in an attempt to improve the quality of the classroom experience, and this is to be commended. This proposal goes further by identifying that learning must not only be an output of theological education, it should also contribute to ongoing outcomes and impact. Students are to enjoy the best possible learning experience so that they can teach and train others. In the light of the LTT, the understanding of "teaching" includes the instruction and training of others. Therefore, faculty are to help students learn so that as graduates they will be able to teach others. Third, in keeping with the above, there is a shift in focus from faculty serving the students, to faculty serving the churches by the way they train students. Faculty lift their sights from the students in front of them to envisage the churches and contexts in which graduates will serve in the

---

44. To achieve the desired input, output, outcome, and impact of integrated theological education requires not just the assessment of students. The curriculum needs to be evaluated for its effectiveness in teaching and learning. See, for example, Harkness, "Role of Academic Leadership," 143–45. Shaw and Jaison go further, arguing for assessment and evaluation at every level of the education process and the life of the theological education institution. See Shaw, 52–58; Jaison, *Towards Vital Wholeness*, 181–85.

future, and ask, "Is what I'm teaching, and how students are learning, going to produce graduates the churches need?" Given that theological education is to serve the church (Principle 2), theological educators are in some measure accountable to the church for the impact graduates have, for good or ill.

The paradigm shift in the role and focus of faculty needs to be supported through faculty development. Traditionally, faculty have required a doctorate. Under this proposal, the role of a lecturer is more complex. As a trainer of trainers, it is a combination of educator, mentor, pastor, parent, and coach, and so requires more sophisticated training. Graham Cheesman identifies that faculty need training, support, and development in four areas:

1. Academic (including the cultivation of right attitudes, breadth and depth of their subject area, and relating study to their spiritual life);
2. Professional (especially as educators);
3. Discipleship (growing in love for God and other people);
4. Ministry (including their skills and stewardship).[45]

Under this helpful framework, developing lecturers as trainers of trainers would involve equipping them across all four areas. The effect would be to enhance integration in the lives of lecturers, so that they can model this for their students. Their academic knowledge would feed the content of what they teach and be matched by the skill of training students to train others as disciples who make disciples, as together lecturer and students serve in ministry. This would require lecturers to keep growing in their own walk with God, ministry capacity and skills, and relational connection with people.

Discussion Questions

1. In your view, what are the strengths and weaknesses of the proposals put forward in this chapter?

2. Do you agree with the proposal that "faculty shift from being scholars and researchers to trainers of trainers"? Why or why not?

3. What aspects of the proposals most closely resonate with your own context?

---

45. Cheesman, "Definitions and Concepts," 48–55.

4. Are there changes you would like to make in the light of what you have read and discussed? What are the opportunities for implementing these changes?

5. What are the top three things you have learned from this book?

Bibliography

Adams, Edward. "The Shape of the Pauline Churches." In *The Oxford Handbook of Ecclesiology*, edited by Paul Avis, 119–46. Oxford: OUP, 2018.
Akin, Daniel L. "The Mystery of Godliness Is Great: Christology in the Pastoral Epistles." In *Entrusted with the Gospel: Paul's Theology in the Pastoral Epistles*, edited by Andreas J. Köstenberger and Terry J. Wilder, 137-52. Nashville: B&H, 2010.
———. "Theology for Church, Worship, and Ministry." In *Theology, Church, and Ministry: A Handbook for Theological Education*, edited by David S. Dockery, 389–410. Nashville: B&H Academic, 2017.
———. "Titus." In *Christ-Centered Exposition: Exalting Jesus in 1 & 2 Timothy and Titus*, edited by David Platt, Tony Merida, and Daniel L. Akin, 225–307. Nashville: B&H, 2013.
Aleshire, Daniel O. *Earthen Vessels: Hopeful Reflections on the Work and Future of Theological Schools*. Grand Rapids: Eerdmans, 2008.
Andria, Solomon. "1 Timothy, 2 Timothy, Titus." In *Africa Bible Commentary*, edited by Tokunboh Adeyemo, 1469–86. Nairobi: WordAlive, 2006.
Aristotle. *Metaphysics*. Translated by H. Tredennick. LCL. Cambridge: HUP, 1933.
———. *Politics*. Translated by H. Rackham. LCL. Cambridge: HUP, 1932.
Asumang, Annang. "Fostering Spiritual Formation at a Distance: Review of the Current Debates, and a Biblically Grounded Proposal for Maximizing Its Effectiveness as Part of Ministerial Formation." *Conspectus* 22, no. 9 (2016): 2–38.
Bailey, Mark L. "The Foundation and Shape of Theological Education." In *Theology, Church, and Ministry*, edited by David S. Dockery, 23–42. Nashville: B&H Academic, 2017.
Ball, Les. "A Thematic History of Theological Education in Australia." In *Theological Education: Foundations, Practices, and Future Directions*, edited by Andrew M. Bain and Ian Hussey, 88–100. Eugene: Wipf & Stock, 2018.
———. *Transforming Theology: Student Experience and Transformative Learning in Undergraduate Theological Education*. Preston: Mosaic Press, 2012.
———. "Where Are We Going?" In *Learning and Teaching Theology: Some Ways Ahead*, edited by Les Ball and James L. Harrison, 11–20. Northcote: Morning Star, 2014.

Ballard, Paul. "The Use of Scripture." In *The Wiley-Blackwell Companion to Practical Theology*, edited by Bonnie J. Miller-McLemore, 163–72. Chichester: Blackwell, 2012.

Banks, Robert. "Paul as Theological Educator: His Original Legacy and Continuing Challenge." In *Learning and Teaching Theology: Some Ways Ahead*, edited by Les Ball and James L. Harrison, 49–56. Northcote: Morning Star, 2014.

———. *Reenvisioning Theological Education: Exploring a Missional Alternative to Current Models*. Grand Rapids: Eerdmans, 1999.

Barclay, John M. G. "Household Networks and Early Christian Economics: A Fresh Study of 1 Timothy 5.3–16." *NTS* 66 (2020): 268–87.

Barentsen, Jack. *Emerging Leadership in the Pauline Mission: A Social Identity Perspective on Local Leadership Development in Corinth and Ephesus*. Princeton Theological Monograph 168. Eugene: Pickwick, 2011.

Bassler, Jouette M. *1 Timothy, 2 Timothy, Titus*. ANTC. Nashville: Abingdon Press, 1996.

Bauckham, R. *Bible and Mission: Christian Witness in a Postmodern World*. Carlisle: Paternoster, 2003.

Beard, Christopher B. "Connecting Spiritual Formation and Adult Learning Theory: An Examination of Common Principles." *CEJ* 14, no. 2 (2017): 247–69.

Beck, David R. "The Linguistic Features of Second Timothy and Its Purpose." In *New Testament Philology: Essays in Honor of David Alan Black*, edited by Melton Bennett Winstead, 159–75. Eugene: Wipf & Stock, 2018.

Belleville, Linda L. "Christology, Greco-Roman Religious Piety, and the Pseudonymity of the Pastoral Epistles." In *Paul and Pseudepigraphy*, edited by Stanley E. Porter and Gregory P. Fewster, 221–43. Leiden: Brill, 2013.

Bernard, J. H. *The Pastoral Epistles*. Thornapple Commentaries. Grand Rapids: Baker, 1980.

Blight, Richard C. *An Exegetical Summary of 1 Timothy*. Dallas: SIL International, 2009.

Bonner, Stanley F. *Education in Ancient Rome: From the Elder Cato to the Younger Pliny*. London: Methuen, 1977.

Bosch, David J. *Transforming Mission: Paradigm Shifts in Theology of Mission*. Maryknoll: Orbis, 1991.

Bray, Gerald L. *The Pastoral Epistles*. ITC. New York: Bloomsbury T&T Clark, 2019.

Brock, Vera. "Integrated Curriculum Design for Holistic Student Development." In *Leadership in Theological Education: Foundations for Curriculum Design*, edited by Fritz Deininger and Orbelina Eguizabal, 281–315. Carlisle: Langham Global Library, 2017.

Browning, Don S. *A Fundamental Practical Theology: Descriptive and Strategic Proposals*. Minneapolis: Fortress, 1991.
Brox, Norbert. *Die Pastoralbriefe*. RNT. Regensburg: Pustet, 1969.
Brynjolfson, Robert W. "Missionary Training and Spirituality: Spiritual Formation in Theological Education." In *Handbook of Theological Education in World Christianity*, edited by Dietrich Werner, David Esterline, Namsoon Kang, and Joshua Raja, 196–202. Oxford: Regnum, 2010.
Cahalan, Kathleen A. "Integration in Theological Education." In *The Wiley-Blackwell Companion to Practical Theology*, edited by Bonnie J. Miller-McLemore, 386–95. Chichester: Blackwell, 2012.
Cahalan, Kathleen A., and James R. Nieman. "Mapping the Field of Practical Theology." In *For Life Abundant: Practical Theology, Theological Education, and Christian Ministry*, edited by Dorothy C. Bass and Craig Dykstra, 62–85. Grand Rapids: Eerdmans, 2008.
Calvin, John. *Institutes of the Christian Religion*. Translated by Ford Lewis Battles. Edited by John T. McNeill. Library of Christian Classics. 2 vols. London: SCM, 1961.
Campbell, R. A. "Identifying the Faithful Sayings in the Pastoral Epistles." *JSNT* 54 (1994): 73–86.
Cannell, Linda. *Theological Education Matters: Leadership Education for the Church*. Newburgh: EDCOT Press, 2006.
———. "Theology, Spiritual Formation and Theological Education: Reflections towards Application." In *Life in the Spirit: Spiritual Formation in Theological Perspective*, edited by Jeffrey P. Greenman and George Kalantzis, 229–49. Downers Grove: IVP, 2010.
Charry, Ellen T. *By the Renewing of Your Minds: The Pastoral Function of Christian Doctrine*. New York: OUP, 1997.
———. "Educating for Wisdom: Theological Studies as a Spiritual Exercise." *Theology Today* 66, no. 3 (2009): 295–308.
Cheesman, Graham. "Competing Paradigms in Theological Education Today." *ERT* 17, no. 4 (1993): 484–99.
———. "Definitions and Concepts of Faculty Development." In *Leadership in Theological Education: Foundations for Faculty Development*, edited by Fritz Deininger and Orbelina Eguizabal, 39–62. Carlisle: Langham Global Library, 2018.
Cicero. *On the Orator*. Translated by E. W. Sutton and H. Rackham. 2 vols., LCL. Cambridge: HUP, 1948.
Cole, Graham A. "Theological Education: A Personalist Perspective." *Journal of Christian Education* 44, no. 3 (2001): 21–31.

Collins, Raymond F. "From Πλρουσιλ to Επιθλνειλ: The Transformation of a Pauline Motif." In *Unity and Diversity in the Gospels and Paul: Essays in Honor of Frank J. Matera*, edited by Christopher W. Skinner and Kelly R. Iverson, 273–99. Atlanta: SBL, 2012.

———. *I & II Timothy and Titus*. NTL. Louisville: Westminster John Knox, 2002.

Collinson, Sylvia. "Making Disciples: An Educational Strategy for Use beyond the Time of Jesus?" *Journal of Christian Education* 43, no. 3 (2000): 7–18.

Conn, Harvie M. *Eternal Word and Changing Worlds: Theology, Anthropology, and Mission in Trialogue*. Phillipsburg: P&R, 1992.

Copan, Victor A. *Saint Paul as Spiritual Director: An Analysis of the Concept of the Imitation of Paul with Implications and Applications to the Practice of Spiritual Direction*. PBM. Milton Keynes: Paternoster, 2007.

Cronshaw, Darren. "Reenvisioning Theological Education and Missional Spirituality." *JATE* 9, no. 1 (2012): 9–27.

Cunningham, Scott. "Assessment beyond the 4bs." In *Is It Working? Researching Context to Improve Curriculum*, edited by Stuart Brooking, 29–36. Carlisle: Langham Global Library, 2018.

Danker, F. W., W. Bauer, W. F. Arndt, and F. W. Gingrich eds. *A Greek-English Lexicon of the New Testament and Other Early Christian Literature*. 3rd ed. Chicago: University of Chicago Press, 2000.

Das, Rupen. *Connecting Curriculum with Context: A Handbook for Context Relevant Curriculum Development in Theological Education*. Carlisle: Langham Global Library, 2015.

———. "Relevance and Faithfulness: Challenges in Contextualizing Theological Education." *InSights Journal for Global Theological Education* 1, no. 2 (2016): 17–29.

Davis, Darin H., and Paul J. Wadell. "Educating Lives for Christian Wisdom." *International Journal of Christianity & Education* 20, no. 2 (2016): 90–105.

de Gruchy, Steve. "Theological Education and Missional Practice: A Vital Dialogue." In *Handbook of Theological Education in World Christianity*, edited by Dietrich Werner, David Esterline, Namsoon Kang, and Joshua Raja, 42–50. Oxford: Regnum, 2010.

Dibelius, Martin, and Hans Conzelmann. *The Pastoral Epistles*. Translated by Phillip Buttolph and Adela Yarbro. Hermeneia. Philadelphia: Fortress, 1972.

Dickson, John P. *Mission-Commitment in Ancient Judaism and in the Pauline Communities*. WUNT 2. Tübingen: Mohr Siebeck, 2003.

Dockery, David S. "Theological Education: An Introduction." In *Theology, Church, and Ministry*, edited by David S. Dockery, 3–22. Nashville: B&H Academic, 2017.

Donelson, Lewis R. "Studying Paul: 2 Timothy as Remembrance." In *SBL Seminar 1997 Papers*, 715–31. Atlanta: Scholars, 1997.

Doornenbal, Robert. *Crossroads: An Exploration of the Emerging-Missional Conversation with a Special Focus on "Missional Leadership" and Its Challenges for Theological Education*. Delft: Eburon, 2012.

Duraisingh, Christopher. "Ministerial Formation for Mission: Implications for Theological Education." *IRM* 81, no. 321 (1992): 33–45.

Edgar, Brian. "The Theology of Theological Education." *ERT* 29, no. 3 (2005): 208–17.

Elengabeka, Elvis. "La Rhétorique de la temporalité dans les épîtres pastorales." In *Perceptions du temps dans la Bible*, edited by Marc Leroy and Martin Staszak, 377–95. Études bibliques. Leuven: Peeters, 2018.

Espinoza, Benjamin D. "Between Text and Context: Practical Theology and the Ministry of Equipping." *CEJ* 14, no. 2 (2017): 391–404.

Esterline, David, Dietrich Werner, Todd Johnson, and Peter Crossing. *Global Survey on Theological Education 2011–2013: Summary of Main Findings*. Report presented to the WCC 10th Anniversary. Busan, 2013.

Everist, Norma Cook, and Craig L. Nessan. "Twelve Pastoral Practices for the Life and Mission of the Church." *Currents in Theology and Mission* 38, no. 5 (2011): 314–16.

Farley, Edward. *Theologia: The Fragmentation and Unity of Theological Education*. Philadelphia: Fortress, 1983.

Fee, Gordon D. *1 & 2 Timothy, Titus*. NIBCNT. Rev. ed. Peabody: Hendrickson, 1988.

Ferdinando, Keith. "Theological Education and Character." *Africa Journal of Evangelical Theology* 27, no. 1 (2008): 45–63.

Fiore, Benjamin. *The Function of Personal Example in the Socratic and Pastoral Epistles*. Analecta Biblica. Rome: Biblical Institute Press, 1986.

———. *The Pastoral Epistles*. Sacra Pagina 12. Collegeville: Liturgical, 2007.

Fleischer, Barbara J. "Mezirow's Theory of Tranformative Learning and Lonergan's Method in Theology: Resources for Adult Theological Education." *JATE* 3, no. 2 (2006): 147–62.

Flett, John G. *The Witness of God: The Trinity, Missio Dei, Karl Barth, and the Nature of Christian Community*. Grand Rapids: Eerdmans, 2010.

Flichy, Odile. "Une Lecture de Tite 1,1–2,15." In *2 Timothy and Titus Reconsidered*, edited by Reimund Bieringer, 111–31. Colloquium Oecumenicum Paulinum. Leuven: Peeters, 2018.

Foord, Martin. "The Elements of a Theology of Theological Education." In *Theological Education: Foundations, Practices, and Future Directions*, edited by Andrew M. Bain and Ian Hussey, 29–43. Eugene: Wipf & Stock, 2018.

Forrest, Benjamin K., and Mark A. Lamport. "Modelling Spiritual Formation from a Distance: Paul's Formation Transactions with the Roman Christians." *CEJ* 10, no. 1 (2013): 110–24.

Francis, Peter. "Developing Genuinely Reflective Ministry Practitioners." In *Theological Education: Foundations, Practices, and Future Directions*, edited by Andrew M. Bain and Ian Hussey, 187–99. Eugene: Wipf & Stock, 2018.

Gaikward, Roger. "Curriculum Development in Theological Education: The Case of Senate of Serampore Colleges in South Asia." In *Handbook of Theological Education in World Christianity*, edited by Dietrich Werner, David Esterline, Namsoon Kang, and Joshua Raja, 263–70. Oxford: Regnum, 2010.

Ghiloni, Aaron J. "Is Formation Education?" *Journal of Christian Education* 54, no. 3 (2011): 29–41.

Gibson, R. J. "The Literary Coherence of 1 Timothy." *RTR* 55, no. 2 (1996): 53–66.

Gillham, Simon. "Growing an Acacia Tree: Towards an African Model of Theological Education." *St Mark's Review* 240, no. 2 (2017): 108–27.

Gloer, W. Hulitt. *1 & 2 Timothy-Titus*. Macon: Smith & Helwys, 2010.

Goheen, Michael G. "A Missional Reading of Scripture for Theological Education and Curriculum." In *Reading the Bible Missionally*, edited by Michael G. Goheen, 299–329. Grand Rapids: Eerdmans, 2016.

Goodall, Norman, ed. *Missions under the Cross: Addresses Delivered at the Enlarged Meeting of the Committee of the International Missionary Council at Willingen, in Germany, 1952; With Statements Issued by the Meeting*. London: Edinburgh House, 1953.

Goodrich, John K. "Overseers as Stewards and the Qualifications for Leadership in the Pastoral Epistles." *ZNW* 104, no. 1 (2013): 1–21.

Gourgues, Michel. *Les Deux Lettres à Timothée; La Lettre à Tite*. Commentaire biblique: Nouveau Testament. Paris: Cerf, 2009.

Graham, Elaine. "The State of the Art: Practical Theology Yesterday, Today, and Tomorrow; New Directions in Practical Theology." *Theology* 120, no. 3 (2017): 172–80.

Griffiths, Jonathan I. *Preaching in the New Testament: An Exegetical and Biblical-Theological Study*. NSBT. London: Apollos, 2017.

Guder, Darrell L. "From Mission and Theology to Missional Theology." *PSB* 24, no. 1 (2003): 36–54.

———. "The Implications of a Missional Hermeneutic for Theological Education." In *Reading the Bible Missionally*, edited by Michael G. Goheen, 285–98. Grand Rapids: Eerdmans, 2016.

———. "*Missio Dei:* Integrating Theological Formation for Apostolic Vocation." *Missiology* 37, no. 1 (2009): 63–74.
Haar, Stephen. "Learning, Formation, and Community: Challenges Facing a Distributed Model of Theological Education." *LTJ* 53, no. 1 (2019): 4–15.
———. "Re-Imagining Theological Education for the Church." *LTJ* 51, no. 1 (2017): 47–59.
Hall, D. "Theological Education as Character Formation?" *Theological Education* 24, Supplement 1 (1988): 53–79.
Hamp, Warren G. "Toward a Pauline Shaping of Pastoral Formation." *LTR* 28 (2016): 11–22.
Harkness, Allan. "De-Schooling the Theological Seminary: An Appropriate Paradigm for Ministerial Formation." *Teaching Theology and Religion* 4, no. 3 (2001): 141–54.
———. "Introduction." In *Tending the Seedbeds: Educational Perspectives on Theological Education in Asia*, edited by Allan Harkness, 7–22. Quezon City: Asia Theological Association, 2010.
———. "Learning Approaches in Theological Education Institutions." *JATE* 9, no. 2 (2012): 139–57.
———. "The Role of Academic Leadership in Designing Transformative Teaching and Learning." In *Leadership in Theological Education: Foundations for Curriculum Design*, edited by Fritz Deininger and Orbelina Eguizabal, 135–75. Carlisle: Langham Global Library, 2017.
Harris, Dana M. "Theological Education and Spiritual Formation." In *Theology, Church, and Ministry*, edited by David S. Dockery, 74–89. Nashville: B&H Academic, 2017.
Hentschel, Anni. *Diakonia im Neuen Testament: Studien zur Semantik unter besonderer Berücksichtigung der Rolle von Frauen*. WUNT 2. Tübingen: Mohr Siebeck, 2007.
Herzer, Jens. "'These Things Are Excellent and Profitable to Everyone' (Titus 3:8): The Kindness of God as Paradigm for Ethics." In *Character Ethics and the New Testament: Moral Dimensions of Scripture*, edited by Robert L. Brawley, 127–40. Louisville: Westminster John Knox, 2007.
Heywood, David. "Educating Ministers of Character: Building Character into the Learning Process in Ministerial Formation." *JATE* 10, no. 1 (2013): 4–24.
———. *Kingdom Learning*. London: SCM, 2017.
Hibbert, Richard, and Evelyn Hibbert. "Addressing the Need for Better Integration in Theological Education." In *Learning and Teaching Theology: Some Ways Ahead*, edited by Les Ball and James L. Harrison, 107–17. Northcote: Morning Star, 2014.
Hill, Graham. *Global Church: Reshaping Our Conversations, Renewing Our Mission, Revitalizing Our Churches*. Downers Grove: IVP, 2016.

Ho, Chiao Ek. "Mission in the Pastoral Epistles." In *Entrusted with the Gospel: Paul's Theology in the Pastoral Epistles*, edited by Andreas J. Köstenberger and Terry J. Wilder, 241–67. Nashville: B&H Academic, 2010.

Hockridge, Diane. "Challenges for Educators Using Online and Distance Education to Prepare Students for Relational Professions." *Distance Education* 34, no. 2 (2013): 142–60.

———. "Reimagining Christian Formation in Online Theological Education." In *Reimagining Christian Education: Cultivating Transformative Approaches*, edited by Johannes M. Luetz, Tony Dowden, and Beverley Norsworthy, 327–43. Singapore: Springer, 2018.

———. "Rethinking Our Approach to Student Formation in Australian Theological Education." In *Theological Education: Foundations, Practices, and Future Directions*, edited by Andrew M. Bain and Ian Hussey, 200–214. Eugene: Wipf & Stock, 2018.

Hodgson, Peter C. *God's Wisdom: Toward a Theology of Education*. Louisville: Westminster John Knox, 1999.

Hoklotubbe, T. Christopher. *Civilized Piety: The Rhetoric of Pietas in the Pastoral Epistles and the Roman Empire*. Waco: Baylor University Press, 2017.

Houlden, J. L. *The Pastoral Epistles: I and II Timothy, Titus*. London: SCM, 1989.

House, Paul R. *Bonhoeffer's Seminary Vision: A Case for Costly Discipleship and Life Together*. Wheaton: Crossway, 2015.

Hultgren, Arland J. "The Pastoral Epistles and the Scriptures of Israel." In *Paul and Scripture*, edited by Stanley E. Porter and Christopher D. Land, 372–90. Leiden: Brill, 2019.

Hume, Bruce. "A Vision for the Good Life: *Shalom* as a *Telos* for Christian Formation in Teaching Theological Reflection." In *Wondering about God Together: Research-Led Learning & Teaching in Theological Education*, edited by Les Ball and Peter G. Bolt, 140–61. Macquarie Park: SCD, 2018.

Hutson, Christopher R. *First and Second Timothy and Titus*. Paideia. Grand Rapids: Baker Academic, 2019.

"ICETE Manifesto on the Renewal of Evangelical Theological Education." *ERT* 8, no. 1 (1984): 136–43.

Jackson, Christopher D. "The Phenomenon of Social Presence in the Pauline Epistles and Its Implication for Practices of Online Education." EdD diss., Southern Baptist Theological Seminary, 2015.

Jaison, Jessy. *Towards Vital Wholeness in Theological Education: Framing Areas for Assessment*. Carlisle: Langham Global Library, 2017.

Johnson, Luke Timothy. *The First and Second Letters to Timothy.* AB. New York: Doubleday, 2001.

Jones, Timothy P., Gabriel Etzel, Christopher Jackson, and John Cartwright. *Teaching the World: Foundations for Online Theological Education.* Nashville: B&H Academic, 2017.

Kelly, J. N. D. *A Commentary on the Pastoral Epistles: I Timothy, II Timothy, Titus.* BNTC. London: A&C Black, 1963.

Kelsey, David H. *Between Athens and Berlin: The Theological Education Debate.* Grand Rapids: Eerdmans, 1993.

Kittel, G., and G. Friedrich, eds. *Theological Dictionary of the New Testament.* Translated by G. W. Bromiley. 10 vols. Grand Rapids: Eerdmans, 1964–1976.

Knight, George William. *The Pastoral Epistles.* NIGTC. Grand Rapids: Eerdmans, 1992.

Köstenberger, Andreas J. "An Investigation of the Mission Motif in the Letters to Timothy and Titus with Implications for the Pauline Authorship of the Pastoral Epistles." *BBR* 29, no. 1 (2019): 49–64.

———. *1–2 Timothy & Titus.* Nashville: B&H, 2017.

Köstenberger, Andreas J., and Terry J. Wilder, eds. *Entrusted with the Gospel: Paul's Theology in the Pastoral Letters.* Nashville: B&H, 2010.

Krause, Deborah. *1 Timothy.* Readings. London: T&T Clark, 2004.

Krejcir, Richard J. "Statistics on Pastors: 2016 Update." Francis A. Schaeffer Institute of Church Leadership Development, 2016. https://files.stablerack.com/webfiles/71795/pastorsstatWP2016.pdf.

Kreminski, Karina, and Michael Frost. "Theological Education for Missional Leadership." In *Theological Education: Foundations, Practices, and Future Directions,* edited by Andrew M. Bain and Ian Hussey, 175–86. Eugene: Wipf & Stock, 2018.

Lau, Andrew Y. *Manifest in Flesh: The Epiphany Christology of the Pastoral Epistles.* WUNT 2. Tübingen: Mohr Siebeck, 1996.

Lindbeck, George. "Spiritual Formation and Theological Education." *Theological Education* 24, Supplement 1 (1988): 10–32.

Lock, Walter. *A Critical and Exegetical Commentary on the Pastoral Epistles: I & II Timothy and Titus.* ICC. Edinburgh: T&T Clark, 1924.

Long, Jude. "Teaching Adults: Insights from Educational Philosophy." *Journal of Christian Education* 53, no. 1 (2010): 49–60.

Lowe, Stephen D., and Mary E. Lowe. "Spiritual Formation in Theological Distance Education: An Ecosystems Model." *CEJ* 7, no. 1 (2010): 85–102.

Ma, Wonsuk. "'Life' in Theological Education and Missional Formation: A Reflection for a New Christian Era." *Transformation* 33, no. 1 (2016): 1–15.

Major, Heather J. "Context Is Key: A Conversation between Biblical Studies, Practical Theology and Missiology." *Foundations* 75, no. 2 (Nov. 2018): 47–61.

Malherbe, Abraham J. "Godliness, Self-Sufficiency, Greed, and the Enjoyment of Wealth: 1 Timothy 6:3–19, Part I." *NovT* 52 (2010): 376–405.

———. "Overseers as Household Managers in the Pastoral Epistles." In *Text, Image, and Christians in the Graeco-Roman World: A Festschrift in Honor of David Lee Balch*, edited by Aliou Cissé Niang and Carolyn Osiek. PTMS, 72–88. Eugene: Pickwick, 2012.

———. "Paraenesis in the Epistle to Titus." In *Early Christian Paraenesis in Context*, edited by J. Starr and T. Engberg-Pedersen, 297–317. Berlin: de Gruyter, 2004.

———. *Paul and the Popular Philosophers*. Minneapolis: Fortress, 1989.

Manomi, Dogara Ishaya. "Salvific, Ethical, and Consummative Appearances in the Pastoral Epistles? A Response to Rob Van Houwelingen." *JSPL* 9, no. 1–2 (2019): 109–17.

Marshall, I. H. *The Pastoral Epistles*. ICC. Edinburgh: T&T Clark, 1999.

Martin, Brice L. "1 Timothy 3:16: A New Perspective." *EvQ* 85, no. 2 (2013): 105–20.

Matera, Frank J. *New Testament Theology*. Louisville: Westminster John Knox, 2007.

Maurice, Lisa. *The Teacher in Ancient Rome: The Magister and His Word*. Lanham: Lexington, 2013.

McEwen, Rhonda M. "Learning That Transforms: For the Sake of His Kingdom." *CEJ* 9, no. 2 (2012): 345–56.

Melick, Rick, and Shera Melick. *Teaching That Transforms: Facilitating Life Change through Adult Bible Teaching*. Nashville: B&H, 2010.

Merkle, Benjamin L. "Ecclesiology in the Pastoral Epistles." In *Entrusted with the Gospel: Paul's Theology in the Pastoral Epistles*, edited by Andreas J. Köstenberger and Terry J. Wilder, 173–98. Nashville: B&H, 2010.

———. *The Elder and Overseer: One Office in the Early Church*. Studies in Biblical Literature 57. New York: Peter Lang, 2003.

———. "Offices, Titles, and Roles: Leadership in Early Church Polity." In *Biblical Leadership: Theology for the Everyday Leader*, edited by Benjamin K. Forrest and Chet Roden, 381–94. Grand Rapids: Kregel, 2017.

Meye, Robert P. "Theological Education as Character Formation." *Theological Education* 24, Supplement 1 (1988): 96–126.

Miller, Sharon L., and Christian Sharen. *(Not) Being There: Online Distance Theological Education*. Auburn Studies 23 (New York: Auburn, 2017). https://auburnseminary.org/report/not-being-there/.

Miller-McLemore, Bonnie J. "The Contributions of Practical Theology." In *The Wiley-Blackwell Companion to Practical Theology*, edited by Bonnie J. Miller-McLemore, 1–20. Chichester: Blackwell, 2012.

———. "Practical Theology and Pedagogy: Embodying Theological Know-How." In *For Life Abundant: Practical Theology, Theological Education, and Christian Ministry*, edited by Dorothy C. Bass and Craig Dykstra, 170–90. Grand Rapids: Eerdmans, 2008.

———. "The Theory–Practice Distinction and the Complexity of Practical Knowledge." *HTS Teologiese Studies/Theological Studies* 72, no. 4 (2016): e1–e8.

Missional Training Center. https://missionaltraining.org.

———. "Theological Education." https://missionaltraining.org/theological-education.

Mounce, William D. *Pastoral Epistles*. WBC. Nashville: Nelson, 2000.

Mutschler, Bernhard. *Glaube in den Pastoralbriefen:* Pistis *als Mitte Christlicher Existenz*. WUNT. Tübingen: Mohr Siebeck, 2010.

Naidoo, Marilyn. "Ministerial Formation of Theological Students through Distance Education." *HTS Teologiese Studies/Theological Studies* 68, no. 2 (2012): 1–8.

———. "The Nature and Application of Formational Learning in the Distance Medium." *HTS Teologiese Studies/Theological Studies* 75, no. 1 (2019): 1–7.

———. "Spiritual Formation in Protestant Theological Institutions." In *Handbook of Theological Education in World Christianity*, edited by Dietrich Werner, David Esterline, Namsoon Kang, and Joshua Raja, 185–95. Oxford: Regnum, 2010.

Neudorfer, Heinz-Werner. *Der erste Brief des Paulus an Timotheus*. HTA. Witten: Brockhaus, 2004.

Newbigin, J. E. Lesslie. *One Body, One Gospel, One World*. London: International Missionary Council, 1958.

———. *The Open Secret: Sketches for a Missionary Theology*. Grand Rapids: Eerdmans, 1978.

Newton, Phillip A. *The Mentoring Church: How Pastors and Congregations Cultivate Leaders*. Grand Rapids: Kregel, 2017.

Ngewa, Samuel M. *1 & 2 Timothy and Titus*. Africa Bible Commentary Series. Nairobi: HippoBooks, 2009.

Nichols, Mark. "The Akadameia as Paradigm for Online Community in Theological Distance Education." *Journal of Christian Education* 54, no. 1 (2011): 5–23.

———. "A Comparison of the Spiritual Participation of On-Campus and Theological Distance Education Students." *JATE* 12, no. 2 (2015): 121–36.

———. "The Formational Experiences of On-Campus and Theological Distance Education Students." *JATE* 13, no. 1 (2016): 18–32.

Noelliste, Dieumeme. "Handmaiden to God's Economy: Biblical Foundations of Theological Education." In *Leadership in Theological Education, Vol. 1: Foundations for Academic Leadership*, edited by Fritz Deininger and Orbelina Eguizabal, 7–31. Carlisle: Langham Global Library, 2017.

Oberlinner, Lorenz. *Die Pastoralbriefe*. HThKNT. 3 vols. Freiburg: Herder, 1994–96.

O'Brien, P. T. *The Letter to the Ephesians*. PNTC. Grand Rapids: Eerdmans, 1999.

O'Donnell, Tim. "The Rhetorical Strategy of 1 Timothy." *CBQ* 79, no. 3 (2017): 455–75.

Osmer, Richard R. *Practical Theology: An Introduction*. Grand Rapids: Eerdmans, 2008.

Ott, Bernhard. *Beyond Fragmentation: Integrating Mission and Theological Education – A Critical Assessment of Some Recent Developments in Evangelical Theological Education*. Oxford: Regnum, 2001.

———. *Understanding and Developing Theological Education*. Carlisle: Langham Global Library, 2016.

Ott, Craig, and Stephen J. Strauss. *Encountering Theology of Mission: Biblical Foundations, Historical Developments, and Contemporary Issues*. Grand Rapids: Baker Academic, 2010.

Oxenham, Marvin. *Character and Virtue in Theological Education: An Academic Epistolary Novel*. ICETE. Carlisle: Langham Global Library, 2019.

———. "A Critical Assessment of the Impact Agenda." In *Is It Working? Researching Context to Improve Curriculum*, edited by Stuart Brooking, 119–27. Carlisle: Langham Global Library, 2018.

Packard Humanities Institute. Available https://inscriptions.packhum.org.

Patrick, Tim. "The Pastoral Offices in the Pastoral Epistles and the Church of England's First Ordinal." In *Paul as Pastor*, edited by Brian S. Rosner, Andrew S. Malone, and Trevor J. Burke, 159–82. London: Bloomsbury, 2018.

Paul, Ian. "Is David Bosch's 'Missio Dei' an Error?" *Psephizo*, 20 November 2017. https://www.psephizo.com/reviews/is-david-boschs-missio-dei-an-error/.

Paver, John E. *Theological Reflection and Education for Ministry*. Aldershot: Ashgate, 2006.

Plato. *Lysis, Symposium, Gorgias*. Translated by W. R. M. Lamb. LCL. Cambridge: HUP, 1975.

Perkins, Larry J. *The Pastoral Letters: A Handbook on the Greek Text*. BHGNT. Waco: Baylor University Press, 2017.

Prior, Michael. *Paul the Letter-Writer and the Second Letter to Timothy.* JSNTSS 23. Sheffield: Sheffield Academic, 1989.
Quinn, Jerome D., and William C. Wacker. *The First and Second Letters to Timothy.* Grand Rapids: Eerdmans, 2000.
Quintilian. *Institutio Oratoria.* Translated by H. E. Butler. 4 vols., LCL. Cambridge: HUP, 1920–1922.
Redalié, Yann. "'Sois un modèle pour les croyants': Timothée, un portrait exhortatif, 1 Tm 4." In *1 Timothy Reconsidered*, edited by Karl Paul Donfried. Colloquium Oecumenicum Paulinum, 87–108. Leuven: Peeters, 2008.
Reddie, Anthony G. "Teaching and Researching Practical Theology: A Liberative Participative Approach to Pedagogy and Qualitative Research." In *Qualitative Research in Theological Education: Pedagogy in Practice*, edited by Mary Clark Moschella and Susan Willhauck, 118–32. London: SCM, 2018.
Roberts, J. J. "Online Learning as a Form of Distance Education: Linking Formation Learning in Theology to the Theories of Distance Education." *HTS Teologiese Studies/Theological Studies* 75, no. 1 (2019): 1–9.
Rogers, P. Alice, and Robert Winstead. "Pedagogical Lessons from Students in Ecclesial Contexts." In *Contextualizing Theological Education*, edited by Theodore Brelsford and P. Alice Rogers, 56–66. Cleveland: Pilgrim, 2008.
Roloff, Jürgen. *Der erste Brief an Timotheus.* EKKNT 15. Zurich: Benziger, 1988.
Root, Andrew. *Christopraxis: A Practical Theology of the Cross.* Minneapolis: Fortress, 2014.
Rosner, Brian S. *Paul and the Law: Keeping the Commandments of God.* NSBT. Nottingham: Apollos, 2013.
Roxburgh, Alan J. "Missional Leadership: Equipping God's People for Mission." In *Missional Church: A Vision for the Sending of the Church in North America*, edited by Darrell L. Guder, 183–220. Grand Rapids: Eerdmans, 1998.
Saarinen, Risto. *The Pastoral Epistles with Philemon & Jude.* Brazos Theological Commentary. Grand Rapids: Brazos, 2008.
Salier, W. H. "Facilitating Student Formation in Tertiary Education." In *God's Exemplary Graduates: Character-Oriented Graduate Attributes in Theological Education*, edited by Peter G. Bolt and Peter Laughlin, 315–32. Macquarie Park: SCD, 2021.
San, Tan Kang. "What Is So Theological about Contextual Mission Training?" In *Contextualisation and Mission Training: Engaging Asia's Religious World*, edited by Jonathan Ingleby, Tan Kang San, and Loun Ling Ling, 1–15. Oxford: Regnum, 2013.
Sands, Edward. "What Is Your Orientation? Perspectives on the Aim of Theological Education." *Journal of Christian Education* 44, no. 3 (2001): 7–18.

Sayler, Gwen B. "The Practice of Biblical and Theological Wisdom." *Currents in Theology and Mission* 38, no. 5 (2011): 327–31.
Schlarb, Egbert. *Die gesunde Lehre: Häresie und Wahrheit im Spiegel der Pastoralbriefe.* MTS. Marburg: N. G. Elwert, 1990.
Schnelle, Udo. *Theology of the New Testament.* Translated by M. Eugene Boring. Grand Rapids: Baker Academic, 2009.
Schreiner, Thomas R. "Overseeing and Serving the Church in the Pastoral and General Epistles." In *Shepherding God's Flock: Biblical Leadership in the New Testament and Beyond*, edited by Benjamin L. Merkle and Thomas R. Schreiner, 89–118. Grand Rapids: Kregel, 2014.
Sharen, Christian A. B., and Eileen R. Campbell-Reid. *Learning Pastoral Imagination: A Five-Year Report on How New Ministers Learn in Practice.* Auburn Studies 21. New York: Auburn Theological Seminary, 2016.
Shaw, Perry. "Holistic and Transformative: Beyond a Typological Approach to Theological Education." *ERT* 40, no. 3 (2016): 205–16.
———. *Transforming Theological Education: A Practical Handbook for Integrative Learning.* Carlisle: Langham Global Library, 2014.
Simpson, Graham. *The Pastoral Epistles: 1-2 Timothy, Titus.* India Commentary on the New Testament. Bengaluru: Primalogue, 2012.
Smith, Claire S. *Pauline Communities as "Scholastic Communities."* WUNT 2. Tübingen: Möhr Siebeck, 2012.
Smith, Craig. A. *Timothy's Task, Paul's Prospect: A New Reading of 2 Timothy.* NTN. Sheffield: Sheffield Phoenix, 2006.
Smith, J. I. "Spiritual Awareness and the Formation of Character." *Theological Education* 24, Supplement 1 (1988): 80–95.
Smith, James K. A. *Desiring the Kingdom: Worship, Worldview, and Cultural Formation.* Grand Rapids: Baker Academic, 2009.
———. *Imagining the Kingdom: How Worship Works.* Grand Rapids: Baker Academic, 2013.
Spicq, Ceslas. *Les Épîtres pastorales.* Études bibliques. 2 vols. Paris: Gabalda, 1969.
———. *Theological Lexicon of the New Testament.* Translated by J. D. Ernest. 3 vols. Peabody: Hendrickson, 1994.
Stache, Kristine. "Formation for the Whole Church: A New/Old Vision of Theological Education in the 21st Century." *Dialog: A Journal of Theology* 53, no. 4 (2014): 286–92.

Stache, Kristine, and Craig L. Nessan. "Adventures into Digital Teaching, Learning, and Formation: A Case Study from Wartburg Theological Seminary." *Journal of Religious Leadership* 17, no. 3 (2017): 20–45.

Starling, David. "The Scribe, the Steward and the Inhabiting Word." In *Theological Education: Foundations, Practices, and Future Directions*, edited by Andrew M. Bain and Ian Hussey, 17–28. Eugene: Wipf & Stock, 2018.

Stepp, Perry L. *Leadership Succession in the World of the Pauline Circle*. NTM 5. Sheffield: Sheffield Phoenix, 2005.

Stettler, Hanna. *Die Christologie der Pastoralbriefe*. WUNT 2. Tübingen: Mohr Siebeck, 1998.

Stirewalt Jr., M. Luther. *Paul the Letter Writer*. Grand Rapids: Eerdmans, 2003.

Swinson, L. Timothy. "Πιστὸς Ὁ Λόγος: An Alternative Analysis." *STR* 7, no. 2 (2016): 57–76.

———. *What Is Scripture? Paul's Use of* Graphe *in the Letters to Timothy*. Eugene: Wipf & Stock, 2014.

Taylor, Steve, and Rosemary Dewerse. "Researching the Future: The Implications of Activist Research for Theological Scholarship in Teaching and Learning." In *Wondering about God Together: Research-Led Learning & Teaching in Theological Education*, edited by Les Ball and Peter G. Bolt, 87–105. Macquarie Park: SCD, 2018.

Tenelshof, Judy. "Encouraging the Character Formation of Future Christian Leaders." *JETS* 42, no. 1 (1999): 77–90.

Thompson, Melinda, and Meri MacLeod. "To the Ends of the Earth: Cultural Considerations for Global Online Theological Education." *Theological Education* 49, no. 2 (2015): 113–25.

Thornton, Dillon T. *Hostility in the House of God: An Investigation of the Opponents in 1 and 2 Timothy*. BBRS. Winona Lake: Eisenbrauns, 2016.

Tomlinson, F. A. "The Purpose and Stewardship Theme within the Pastoral Epistles." In *Entrusted with the Gospel: Paul's Theology in the Pastoral Letters*, edited by Andreas J. Köstenberger and Terry J. Wilder, 52–83. Nashville: B&H, 2010.

Towner, Philip H. "Christology in the Letters to Timothy and Titus." In *Contours of Christology in the New Testament*, edited by Richard N. Longenecker, 219–44. Grand Rapids: Eerdmans, 2005.

———. *The Goal of Our Instruction: The Structure of Theology and Ethics in the Pastoral Epistles*. JSNTS 24. Sheffield: JSOT Press, 1989.

———. *The Letters to Timothy and Titus*. NICNT. Grand Rapids: Eerdmans, 2006.

Tracy, David. *The Analogical Imagination: Christian Theology and the Culture of Pluralism.* London: SCM, 1981.

———. "Can Virtue Be Taught? Education, Character, and the Soul." *Theological Education* 24, Supplement 1 (1988): 33–52.

Trebilco, Paul. *The Early Christians in Ephesus from Paul to Ignatius.* Grand Rapids: Eerdmans, 2007.

Treier, Daniel J. *Virtue and the Voice of God: Towards Theology as Wisdom.* Grand Rapids: Eerdmans, 2006.

Vanhoozer, K. J. "From Bible to Theology." In *Theology, Church, and Ministry*, edited by David S. Dockery, 233–56. Nashville: B&H Academic, 2017.

Van Houwelingen, Rob. "The Meaning of Ἐπιφανεία in the Pastoral Epistles." *JSPL* 9, no. 1–2 (2019): 89–108.

Van Rheenan, Gailyn. "Syncretism and Contextualization: The Church on a Journey Defining Itself." In *Contextualization and Syncretism: Navigating Cultural Currents*, edited by Gailyn Van Rheenan, 1–29. Pasadena: William Carey Library, 2006.

Veiling, Terry A. "'Practical Theology': A New Sensibility for Theological Education." *Pacifica* 11, no. 2 (1998): 195–210.

———. *Practical Theology: "On Earth as It Is in Heaven."* Maryknoll: Orbis, 2005.

Wall, Robert W., and Richard B. Steele. *1 & 2 Timothy and Titus.* Two Horizons New Testament Commentary. Grand Rapids: Eerdmans, 2012.

Ward, Pete. *Introducing Practical Theology: Mission, Ministry, and the Life of the Church.* Grand Rapids: Baker, 2017.

Weiser, Alfons. *Der zweite Brief an Timotheus.* EKKNT 16. Zurich: Benziger, 2003.

White, Adam G. *Where Is the Wise Man? Graeco-Roman Education as a Background to the Divisions in 1 Corinthians 1–4.* LNTS 536. London: Bloomsbury T&T Clark, 2015.

Wickett, Reg. "Adult Learning Theories and Theological Education." *JATE* 2, no. 2 (2005): 153–61.

Wieland, George M. "Grace Manifest: Missional Church in the Letter to Titus." *Stimulus* 13, no. 1 (2005): 8–11.

Wilson, Beth L. "Authentic Leadership: Paul's Instructions to Titus." *Journal of Biblical Perspectives in Leadership* 8, no. 1 (2018): 202–12.

Winter, B. W. "Providentia for the Widows of 1 Timothy 5:3–16." *TynBul* 39 (1988): 83–99.

Witherington, Ben. *Letters and Homilies for Hellenized Christians.* Vol. 1. Downers Grove: IVP Academic, 2006.

Wolfe, B. Paul. "The Sagacious Use of Scripture." In *Entrusted with the Gospel: Paul's Theology in the Pastoral Epistles*, edited by Andreas J. Köstenberger and Terry J. Wilder, 199–218. Nashville: B&H, 2010.

Wolter, M. "Der Apostel und sein Schüler: 2 Timotheus 1,1–18." In *2 Timothy and Titus Reconsidered*, edited by Reimund Bieringer, 17–37. Leuven: Peeters, 2018.

Woodward, James, and Stephen Pattison. "An Introduction to Pastoral and Practical Theology." In *The Blackwell Reader in Pastoral and Practical Theology*, edited by James Woodward and Stephen Pattison. Oxford: Blackwell, 2000.

Wright, Christopher J. H. *The Mission of God: Unlocking the Bible's Grand Narrative*. Nottingham: IVP, 2006.

Wright, David C. "'Integration' in the Ancient World: An Anachronistic Concept?" In *God's Exemplary Graduates: Character-Oriented Graduate Attributes in Theological Education*, edited by Peter G. Bolt and Peter Laughlin, 22–31. Macquarie Park: SCD, 2021.

Xenophon. *Cyropadeia*. Translated by W. Miller. LCL. London: Heinemann, 1914.

Yarbrough, Robert W. *The Letters to Timothy and Titus*. PNTC. Grand Rapids: Eerdmans, 2018.

Young, Curtis J. "Transformational Learning in Ministry." *CEJ* 10, no. 2 (2013): 322–38.

Zamfir, Korinna. *Men and Women in the Household of God: A Contextual Approach to Roles and Ministries in the Pastoral Epistles*. NTOA/SUNT 103. Göttingen: Vandenhoeck & Ruprecht, 2013.

ICETE is a global community, sponsored by nine regional networks of theological schools, to enable international interaction and collaboration among all those engaged in strengthening and developing evangelical theological education and Christian leadership development worldwide.

The purpose of ICETE is:
1. To promote the enhancement of evangelical theological education worldwide.
2. To serve as a forum for interaction, partnership and collaboration among those involved in evangelical theological education and leadership development, for mutual assistance, stimulation and enrichment.
3. To provide networking and support services for regional associations of evangelical theological schools worldwide.
4. To facilitate among these bodies the advancement of their services to evangelical theological education within their regions.

Sponsoring associations include:
Africa: Association for Christian Theological Education in Africa (ACTEA)

Asia: Asia Theological Association (ATA)

Caribbean: Caribbean Evangelical Theological Association (CETA)

Europe: European Evangelical Accrediting Association (EEAA)

Euro-Asia: Euro-Asian Accrediting Association (E-AAA)

Latin America: Association for Evangelical Theological Education in Latin America (AETAL)

Middle East and North Africa: Middle East Association for Theological Education (MEATE)

North America: Association for Biblical Higher Education (ABHE)

South Pacific: South Pacific Association of Evangelical Colleges (SPAEC)

www.icete-edu.org

Langham Literature and its imprints are a ministry of Langham Partnership.

Langham Partnership is a global fellowship working in pursuit of the vision God entrusted to its founder John Stott –

> *to facilitate the growth of the church in maturity and Christ-likeness through raising the standards of biblical preaching and teaching.*

Our vision is to see churches in the Majority World equipped for mission and growing to maturity in Christ through the ministry of pastors and leaders who believe, teach and live by the word of God.

Our mission is to strengthen the ministry of the word of God through:
- nurturing national movements for biblical preaching
- fostering the creation and distribution of evangelical literature
- enhancing evangelical theological education

especially in countries where churches are under-resourced.

Our ministry

Langham Preaching partners with national leaders to nurture indigenous biblical preaching movements for pastors and lay preachers all around the world. With the support of a team of trainers from many countries, a multi-level programme of seminars provides practical training, and is followed by a programme for training local facilitators. Local preachers' groups and national and regional networks ensure continuity and ongoing development, seeking to build vigorous movements committed to Bible exposition.

Langham Literature provides Majority World preachers, scholars and seminary libraries with evangelical books and electronic resources through publishing and distribution, grants and discounts. The programme also fosters the creation of indigenous evangelical books in many languages, through writer's grants, strengthening local evangelical publishing houses, and investment in major regional literature projects, such as one volume Bible commentaries like *The Africa Bible Commentary* and *The South Asia Bible Commentary*.

Langham Scholars provides financial support for evangelical doctoral students from the Majority World so that, when they return home, they may train pastors and other Christian leaders with sound, biblical and theological teaching. This programme equips those who equip others. Langham Scholars also works in partnership with Majority World seminaries in strengthening evangelical theological education. A growing number of Langham Scholars study in high quality doctoral programmes in the Majority World itself. As well as teaching the next generation of pastors, graduated Langham Scholars exercise significant influence through their writing and leadership.

To learn more about Langham Partnership and the work we do visit **langham.org**

www.ingramcontent.com/pod-product-compliance
Lightning Source LLC
Chambersburg PA
CBHW070613170426
43200CB00012B/2679